DELINEATIONS
of
GLOUCESTERSHIRE

DELINEATIONS

OF THE

COUNTY OF GLOUCESTER.

Drawn & Eng.d by J. & T. S. Storer.   Pub.d by Sherwood Jones & C.o Oct.r 1, 1824.

DELINEATIONS *of* GLOUCESTERSHIRE

VIEWS OF THE PRINCIPAL SEATS
OF NOBILITY & GENTRY

J.N. Brewer
Engravings by J. & H.S. Storer

NONSUCH

First published 1825
Copyright © in this edition 2005
Nonsuch Publishing Ltd

Nonsuch Publishing Limited
The Mill, Brimscombe Port, Stroud, Gloucestershire, GL5 2QG
www.nonsuch-publishing.com

British Library Cataloguing in Publication Data.
A catalogue record for this book is available from the British Library.

ISBN 1-84588-067-6

Typesetting and origination by Nonsuch Publishing Limited
Printed in Great Britain by Oaklands Book Services Limited

Contents

INTRODUCTION
TO THE MODERN EDITION

THE royal and ancient city of Gloucester, founded originally by the Britons, became in the wake of the Roman retirement one of the principal cities of the kingdom of Mercia. It most likely took its name from a ruling prince by the name of Gloew, whose charge at the time was the country of which Gloucester was capital. This prince has since become 'honoured with posterity, in imparting a permanent name to so fair a city, and to a county so richly endowed by nature and improved by art.'

So it was that Gloucestershire came into being, according to celebrated novelist and topographer J.N. Brewer in his passionate and finely wrought *Delineations of Gloucestershire*. As with his other works, including the *Beauties of England and Wales*, and the much-vaunted *Beauties of Ireland*, Brewer captures in this volume something of the essence of an age. The characters which the author invokes to tell his tale are the stately homes and castles of this historic county, from the majesty of Badminton House in the south-east, seat of the Duke of Beaufort K.G., to Blaise Castle, and High Grove in the hamlet of Charlton.

Each of the homes, estates and manors to which the reader is introduced is evoked with a vigour and precision which is this author's particular skill. The research into the elements of history and design is matched only by the clarity with which it is presented. In this, Brewer's efforts have been supplemented by the unarguable quality of the engravings with which this volume is illustrated. These engravings are the work of the lauded artists J. & H.S. Storer, engravings which are based on the artists' own original drawings. They bring to this piece a vibrancy and immediacy which cannot fail to captivate.

Brewer also makes particular reference to the local and historical knowledge of his patrons, of which he availed to great effect. From the patronage of His Royal Highness William Frederick, Duke of Gloucester, which was proffered and gratefully accepted, to the 'literary taste and polished urbanity' of the Right Honourable Charles Bathurst, Brewer has been allowed to deepen and enrich his *Delineations* through a heightened awareness of historical context and significance. A comprehensive history of Badminton House, for example, explores the connections with the sport to which it gave its name; though it is a game played in various guises, and since ancient times, it was a wet day in Gloucestershire that first prompted the Duke and his guests to first play the game indoors. And thus Badminton was born; it was simply an accident of time that the sport was not known as 'Madminturne', as this estate was recorded in the Domesday Book.

The heritage of High Grove, now known as Highgrove and residence of the Prince of Wales since 1980, takes its place among its peers. The quality of the views of this neo-classical manor house are aptly recommended by the author for 'the hospitable purposes of a family of high respectability.'

Although most of the houses Brewer examines still remain, in splendid defiance of changing times, an added piquancy is added by those that exist no longer. Alderley House, for example, was torn down in 1859. The houses in the centre of Cirencester also fell foul of progress in the nineteenth century. And, of course, The Ridge, too, has gone, following the spectacular and devastating fire which followed Edward Sheppard's equally spectacular bankruptcy in 1837.

As we can see in the variation of spelling throughout, this is a contemporary work, first penned by Brewer in 1825. All such variations have been preserved within this volume, offering, as they do, such a quality of time and place. What emerges is a finely crafted tapestry of the time, capturing a moment from a golden age in Gloucestershire's past. It is a work of very real beauty that should stand the test of passing age at least as well as the stately homes from which it draws its inspiration.

James Norris Brewer's literary talent was shaped over the course of the early nineteenth century by his works of fiction as well as his topographical studies. His many romances, including *A Winter's Tale*, and *The Witch of Ravensworth*, are exemplary of Brewer's descriptive talent, a talent which make *Delineations of Gloucestershire* such an engaging work.

Preface

THE rich field for graphic illustration presented by the county of Gloucester, cannot fail of being highly appreciated by those who are familiar, either through residence or travel, with its numerous seats, many of which present impressive examples of domestic and castellated architecture, aided by the most pleasing varieties of picturesque scenery. It may not be unnecessary to observe that an undertaking, embracing a collective display of the mansions and other interesting subjects in a district so peculiarly fertile in pictorial objects, has not been attempted since the labours of Sir Robert Atkyns, and the publication by Mr. Rudder, the former and most comprehensive work was composed early in the 18th century. On completing this volume of "Delineations of Gloucestershire," the proprietors are induced to trust that their efforts to render it worthy of adoption in the County of Gloucester, and in the libraries of Topographical collectors generally, have not been entirely unsuccessful. The county has been visited and carefully examined. The whole of the Views are engraved from Original Drawings, and no labour has been spared in their execution; whilst much novelty of intelligence is afforded in the Literary Descriptions. The Artists and the Author have great pleasure in acknowledging their obligations to the following noblemen and gentlemen:—

To His Royal Highness William Frederick, Duke of Gloucester, for the honour of his patronage, and other condescending marks of attention. To His Grace the Duke of Beaufort, for the honour of a most polite reception at Badminton, and for much information then afforded by His Grace in regard to that noble seat. To the Right Honourable William Wyndham Grenville, Lord Grenville, their acknowledgements are due for his gratifying acquiescence in their wishes. They are likewise equally indebted to the Right Reverend Christopher Bethel, Lord Bishop of Gloucester. The literary taste and polished urbanity of the Right Honourable Charles Bathurst are so well known, that it would be matter of surprise if the importance of a work on the subject of the county in which that gentleman chiefly resides, was not materially enhanced by his knowledge and unreserved communications; these were made additionally valuable by the manner in which they were conferred. To the Misses Milligan, of Cotswold, particular expressions of gratitude are due for their polite attentions and valuable information.

Very considerable aid has been liberally afforded during the progress of the work by Sir Berkeley William Guise, Bart. M.P.; Honourable Thomas Seymour Bathurst; John. S. Harford, Esq. D.C.L., Sir Harford Jones, Bart.; Sir James Musgrave, Bart; Daniel Cave, Esq. M.A.; Sir Thomas-Crawley Boevey, Bart.; Michael Hicks Beach, Esq.; R.H. Blagdon Hale, Esq.; David Ricardo, Esq.; J. Howell, Esq.; J. Delafield Phelps, Esq.; Ed. Palling Caruthers, Esq.; Wᴹ. Croome, Esq.; W. H. Baillie, Esq.; Lewis Clutterbuck, Esq.; Philip Protheroe, Esq.; H. C. Clifford, Esq.; J. Wyattville, Esq.; Thomas Turner, Esq.; J. H. Byles, Esq.; R. W. Huntley, Esq.; Edward Sheppard, Esq.; T. Jones, Esq.; and the Rev. M. F. Townsend. The Rev. T. D. Fosbroke, the erudite author of a "History of Gloucestershire," and other works well known to the public, with a degree of liberality that cannot be too much commended, contributed copious intelligence on every subject concerning which the aid of his superior local knowledge was requested.

WESTGATE STREET, GLOUCESTER.

I

Gloucester

THE antient and respectable City of Gloucester is situated in the north-western part of the county on which it bestows a name, and upon the eastern borders of the river Severn. If Gloucester possessed no other attraction than its Cathedral, the visiter, imbued with antiquarian taste, must deem the labour of a journey well repaid, by the examination of that beautiful structure; but the city presents numerous additional subjects, of high interest with the lover of topographical detail and historical anecdote.

Gloucester was, undoubtedly, founded by the Britons, and it is observed, in the very able commentary recently published on the Itinerary of Richard of Cirencester, that vestiges are still to be traced of a road, appearing to be British, which commenced on the coast of Devon, and passed through this place in its way to the northern parts of the island. By the founders this city was named CAER GLOEW, or GLOW; a mode of designation by which it is still recognised in Wales. As usual, various etymologies have been employed in explaining an appellation, concerning the adoption of which no satisfactory historical data are known to exist. By many writers the word Gloew is here received in its adjective signification; namely, *Bright, Fair,* or *Splendid*; but, in the "Beauties of England" it is very plausibly contended that the word does not, in this instance, stand for the expression of a quality but a person. A prince named GLOEW, as we are told by the authors of that work, appears to have lived at the commencement of the Roman period of British history, and to have ruled over the country of which this city was the capital. If these latter writers be correct, the British prince is sufficiently honoured with posterity, in imparting a permanent name to so fair a city, and to a county so richly endowed by nature and improved by art.

It is believed that Caer Glow yielded to the Roman arms, under Aulus Plautius, about the year 44 of the Christian era. By Richard of Cirencester it is mentioned as one of the nine colonial cities of the Romans; and various traces of that august people have been discovered at different periods. Among these are tessellated pavements, and other vestiges of buildings, including the shaft of a mutilated Doric column; coins; funeral urns and other relics of sepulture; pieces of amphoræ; a brass lamp; a brass patera, with a handle; a small ornamented bell; and a statera, or balance, composed of brass.

The most recent discovery of Roman antiquities took place a few months since, on the border of the Ermyn Street, now converted in this neighbourhood into a turnpike road. Early in the month of March 1824, as workmen were employed in digging the foundation of a house, adjoining the road at *Wotton,* forming a part of the suburbs of Gloucester, they found, two feet below the surface of the earth, a monumental stone, about four feet long and three feet wide, on which is carved, in alto-relievo, the representation of a Roman soldier on horseback, in the act of striking with a spear a prostrate Briton. The conqueror has a legionary sword on his side.

The prostrate figure represents a man in a rude, and almost savage, state of society; but, although beaten down and perishing, he resists to the last; and lifts, in unavailing vengeance, a weapon of offence bearing much resemblance to the instrument which antiquaries usually term a celt. At each corner of the upper part of the stone are the head and feet of a lion; and, at the top, is a figure having human head and breasts, with the legs of a beast and clawed feet. Under the principal emblematic carving is the following inscription:

RVFVS . SITA . EQVES . CHO . VI
TRACVM . ANN . XL . STIP . XXII
HEREDES . EXS . TEST . E . CVRAVE
H S E

Rufus Sita, of the 6th cohort of Thracian cavalry, aged 40, had
served 22 years.
His heirs caused this to be made according to his will.
Let this be sacred!

Near the stone was found an unornamented vase, filled with fragments of bones, in a very sound state, mixed with earth and dust, as if the whole were sweepings from what remained of the pile of cremation.

A second stone was also found near the above, but in a mutilated condition. On it is inscribed,

XX SLIVI SATVRNINI SIPENDIORVM XIII ORVM MXXXX.

Many urns, filled with ashes and fragments of bones which had passed through the fire, were discovered at the same time and place; and in the adjacent fields were found numerous Roman coins, chiefly of *Tiberius, Claudius*, and *Nero*. These are now in the possession of G. W. Counsel, Esq. of Gloucester.

Under the Romans the name of this place assumed a Latin termination, and became *Glevum*. The exact situation of the Roman Glevum has not been determined by antiquarian investigation. Some writers have supposed that the tract now called *King's Holm* was the site of the Roman colony; but we are decidedly of opinion with Mr. Rudge, that "the present plan of Gloucester," as relates to its principal parts, "nearly corresponds with what it was in the time of the Romans;" and we presume that it will not be necessary to adduce any other foundation for this opinion, than the fact of tessellated pavements, and other indisputable remains of Roman buildings, having been repeatedly discovered in the four principal streets.

When the Romans, retiring from Britain, gave place to a new race of conquerors, Gloucester became one of the fifteen cities which composed the kingdom of Mercia. According to the venerable historian Bede, this was esteemed, towards the commencement of the eighth century, one of the finest cities in the island. By the Saxons the name was changed to *Gleau-cestre*, whence, with a slight variation of orthography, is evidently derived the existing appellation.

That Gloucester was a place of considerable importance at the period of the Norman conquest, is evinced by the circumstance of William I. having frequently held his court here, during the festive ceremonials of Christmas. The extent of the city, and the staple article of its trade, in the latter years of the eleventh century, are satisfactorily shewn by the record termed Domesday. The number of houses at the date of that record was not less than 255, containing, at the average of ten persons to a house, a population of above 2500. Among the dues paid by the citizens, in the time of Edward the Confessor, the principal articles, rendered in kind, were "thirty-six *dicres of iron*, each of ten bars; and a hundred *iron rods*, drawn out for nails of the king's ships."

Amongst other memorable events in the history of Gloucester, it must be mentioned that the inhabitants were zealous in their attachment to the cause of the Empress Maud, who resided for some time in the castle of this city, whilst engaged in opposing the usurpation of Stephen. In this fortress Maud had the temporary triumph of receiving, as a prisoner, her formidable rival, after his defeat in the vicinity of Lincoln. Henry II. held a great council here, in 1175 and Henry III. was crowned in the abbey-church, A.D. 1216. The last-named sovereign retained, through life, a constant partiality for the city of his inauguration, and often held his troubled court within its loyal and protecting walls. The pages of topography are, however, replete with proofs that such marks of distinction, although flattering to the honest pride of the citizens, were fatally injurious to their prosperity. Thus, whilst we contemplate Gloucester as the favoured scene of regal pomp, in the unsettled ages briefly subsequent to the entry of the Normans, we view the far-famed city merely as a military post, in which commerce was neglected and tranquillity unknown.

The royal favour was continued to Gloucester during the calamitous season in which Edward II. wore the crown; and the second Richard, in a time equally noxious to the public interests, held here a factious and unprofitable parliament. Richard III. repaired, immediately after his coronation, to the city which had afforded him a ducal title; and from this place it is said that he sent an order to the governor of the Tower of London, for the murder of the nephew, whom he had deposed, and the brother of that youthful prince. The last parliament assembled here was summoned by Henry V. in the year 1420.

The most important event in the annals of Gloucester, relating to times comparatively modern, is the large share it bore in the intestine military operations of the seventeenth century. It will be recollected that the spirited, yet deliberate and firm, opposition of the inhabitants to the royal cause, is generally believed to have imparted decision to the wavering, and confidence to those who had already taken their side, throughout the whole of the agitated kingdom. Sir Robert Atkyns observes, that "the unfortunate SIEGE OF THIS CITY gave a stand to the king's victorious army, which being raised, it turned the state of the war, and the king could never after obtain success."

Our limits restrain us from attempting even an abridged account of the memorable siege of Gloucester, which lasted nearly a month, the king commanding in person the assailants, whilst the city was placed under the military government of Lieut. Colonel Massie. So few particulars, however, chiefly of a character strictly topographical, may be presented; and for these we are principally indebted to the very curious "Historicall Relation" of the military government of Colonel Massie, by John Corbet, lately reprinted, and forming, in the reprint, part of a work highly honourable to the county, entitled "Bibliotheca Gloucestrensis."

The inhabitants had declared for the Parliament early in the year 1641, at which time they raised a company of volunteers, procured cannon, and strengthened their fortifications. After a disregarded summons to surrender from Prince Rupert, the city was invested by a royal army, the command of which was taken by the king in person, August 10th, 1643. The place was defended, amidst numberless trials and privations, until the 8th of September following; on which day it was relieved by 10,000 men, under the Earl of Essex.

The strength of the garrison, when the siege commenced, consisted in about 1500 men, provided with little artillery, and no more than forty barrels of gunpowder. "The works," says

N.W. VIEW OF THE CITY OF GLOUCESTER

Corbet, "were of a large compasse, and not halfe perfect. From the south gate eastward, almost to the north port," the city was defended by remains of the ancient wall; and "thence to the north gate with a slender work upon a low ground. Upon the lower part of the city, from the north to the west gate, there was no antient defence, but a small work newly raysed, with the advantage of marish grounds without. From the west towards the south gate, along the river side, was no more defence than the river itself, and the meadows beyond. From the castle to the south port was a firme and lofty work, to command the high ground in the suburbs."

The zeal with which the inhabitants espoused the cause of defence, is curiously commemorated by the fact of the women and children having laboured in completing the fortifications. The courage of the females of Gloucester during this memorable siege is, indeed, repeatedly, and most honourably, noticed by contemporary writers. By Corbet it is mentioned that, in the times of greatest danger, "the usual outcryes of women were not heard;" and Dorney, town-clerk of Gloucester, in his "Briefe and Exact Relation" of the most remarkable passages in the siege, observes that the "women and maides wrought, in fetching in turfe from the little meade, for the repair of the works," in the very face of a body of the enemy's horse!

The whole of the suburbs, consisting of 241 houses, besides inferior buildings, were burned, or pulled down, by order of the governor and council of war. "By burning of the suburbs," said the advocates of that measure, "the city is a garment without skirts, which we were willing to part withal, lest our enemies should sit upon them." In the petition for indemnification, afterwards preferred by the mayor, burgesses, and other inhabitants, it is said that the suburbs comprised a full third part of the city; and the damage was proved to have amounted to upwards of £26,000.

As a natural consequence of the conspicuous part the inhabitants had taken in the civil war, the walls of the city were razed, by order of government, shortly after the Restoration. The principal gates, however, which were four in number, remained standing until years near the conclusion of the eighteenth century.

The most memorable event in recent times is the visit with which the city was honoured by his late Majesty, George III. in the year 1788. The present King, when Prince of Wales, also conferred on Gloucester the honour of a visit, October 5th, 1807; on which day his Royal Highness partook of a dinner with the members of the corporation.

The City of Gloucester is seated on a gentle eminence, at the western base of which flows the river Severn. The plan of the city comprehends four principal streets, inclining nearly to the four cardinal points of the compass. These are uniformly of a good width; and, as each lies on an easy descent, a desirable and most agreeable cleanliness of aspect is maintained with little effort. Considerable improvements have been effected within the last half-century; and the domestic buildings (which are chiefly composed of brick), although deficient in regularity, are of a character highly respectable, and many are capacious and handsome structures. We present a View of the part of the city termed Westgate Street showing in the distance the church dedicated to *St. Nicholas.*

From the principal streets diverge many avenues of a minor character, some of which require, and probably will obtain, the hand of improvement at no distant period. The chief streets are well paved, and the best shops are lighted with gas. The whole of the city is chiefly with water conducted through pipes from reservoirs on *Robin's-wood Hill*, an eminence of a conical form, rising from the vale, at the distance of about two miles from Gloucester, towards the south. This city is much famed for salubrity of air, and the country in its vicinity is invariably pleasing, and in several parts picturesque. From these, and other inducements connected with the increasing prosperity of the inhabitants, considerable augmentations are taking place in several suburban directions; and many of the buildings, either completed or in progress, are suited to the occupation of respectable private families, to whom the immediate neighbourhood of this city holds out numerous advantages as a place of residence.

From several points of observation the various buildings of the city, crowned magnificently with the Cathedral-church, compose into a fine and attractive pictorial group; but, perhaps, at no point are the principal objects displayed to greater advantage than at that which we have selected for the VIEW which accompanies this part of our work. Our position is taken on the western bank of the river Severn, and on the path leading to Maisemore. The most prominent buildings here seen are the *Cathedral*; the parochial churches of *St. Michael, St. Nicholas*, and *St. Mary de Lode*; the *Shire Hall*; and the *New Bridge*, over the Severn. In the distance is perceived the elevation termed *Robin's-wood Hill.*

The principal trade of Gloucester, independent of the local traffic common to most English towns, is derived from the navigation of the Severn; from the hemp and flax-dressing business; and from the manufacture of pins; which last-named branch of industry is, we believe, carried on here to a greater extent than in any other place. The public amusements are conducted on a liberal scale, and consist of theatrical exhibitions and assemblies for dancing; to which must be added the *Musical Festival*, established by the members of the choirs of Gloucester, Worcester, and Hereford, and aided by the most eminent performers of London. The meetings are held yearly, and alternately in each of those cities.

Gloucester gives the title of Duke to his Royal Highness William-Frederick, whose father, Prince William-Henry, brother to his late Majesty, was created Duke of Gloucester, by patent, November 10, 1764. It is internally governed by a mayor; twelve aldermen (out of whom the mayor is chosen); a high steward; a recorder; town-clerk; two sheriffs; a common council, &c. The high stewards have generally been persons of distinguished eminence, and that office is at present filled by his Royal Highness the Duke of Gloucester. The city returns two members to the Imperial Parliament, who are chosen by the burgesses and freemen.

Among the PUBLIC BUILDINGS of Gloucester the CATHEDRAL is, in every respect, entitled to primary notice. This structure is, in parts, of almost unrivalled beauty; and, as a whole, is a noble and venerable object, calculated to elicit the admiration equally of the architectural antiquary amid the spectator of a more general taste for the sublime and picturesque. It is with a feeling of surprise, although aware of the munificence with which ecclesiastical architecture was encouraged in past ages, that we find this extensive and splendid pile not to have been originally designed as a cathedral, but merely as an abbey-church. The abbey of Gloucester was founded by Wolfere, King of Mercia, about the year 762. After a long course of prosperity and distinction, that religious foundation was dissolved on the 2nd of January, 1540; and King Henry VIII. in the following year, created Gloucester the see of a bishop, bestowing on the diocess the church of the dissolved abbey, as a cathedral. The gift was worthy of a king; and the inhabitants in general, as well as the clergy, its more immediate guardians, have been so laudably sensible of the value of this superb ornament of the city, that when Gloucester suffered in almost every other part, during the siege in the seventeenth century, especial care was bestowed on the preservation of this august pile, and it remained free from material injury amidst all the havoc of warfare, and the more threatening discordance of religious opinions. The antiquary will wish that the same liberality had been evinced by the early reformers, who mutilated, or utterly destroyed, with indiscriminating severity, the statues of saints and benefactors, which formerly enriched many parts of the building.

The cathedral stands in a spacious area, well calculated to display its numerous excellencies. The exterior is now wholly in the pointed style, although of different ages; but the fabric presents, within a copious variety of the several modes of ecclesiastical architecture used in England, commencing with the circular (Anglo-Saxon or Norman), and embracing, in the plenitude of its examples, the last refinements of the pointed, or Gothic.

The *central tower* was erected after the designs, and partly under the direction, of Abbot Sebroke, who presided over the abbey of St. Peter from 1453 to 1457. It is conspicuous for lightness of character; for symmetry of proportions; and richness, without redundancy, of ornamental particulars. The tower is divided into two stories, and has, at the top, a battlement of open work, surmounted by four pinnacles, perforated into numerous small arches, and terminating in foliated finials. We cannot avoid directing the attention of those who can appreciate *the picturesque of architecture*, to the following remark by Mr. Dallaway, the correctness of which we have ascertained, with feelings of satisfaction that we should vainly endeavour to express. "The extremely beautiful effect of large masses of architecture, *by moonlight*, may be considered as a kind of optical deception. Thus seen, the TOWER OF THIS CATHEDRAL acquires a degree of lightness, so superior to that which it shows under the meridian sun, that it no longer appears to be of human construction."

On entering the cathedral a sentiment of reverence, the most grateful, is excited by the august simplicity and massy grandeur of the NAVE, which is in the circular style of architecture, and was chiefly built by Abbot Serlo, in 1089, and the eleven following years. On each side are eight ponderous round columns, with semicircular arches above, bounded by large zigzag and other mouldings. The vaulting is ribbed with simple cross-springers.

Between the nave and the choir was, until lately, a screen; designed by Kent, which was lamentably discordant with every style observable in antient ecclesiastical architecture. We are happy to have the opportunity of observing that an erection, so offensive to good taste, is now removed, and in its place has been constructed a screen, which, although heavy, and capable of improvements, is still of a simple and more consistent character.

The CHOIR was built between the years 1330 and 1457. This far-famed example of the pointed style, in its most luxuriant stage of beauty, previous to the meretricious redundance of embellishment, amidst which it sank and passed away, has been emphatically said to "include every perfection to which the Gothic had attained during the fifteenth century." Its beauty is, indeed, transcendent, dazzling, and fascinating! The effect is obviously, and greatly, increased by the abruptness of contrast between this highly decorated portion of the church, and the simple but sublime part towards the west.

The cell-work is exquisitely fine. The cross-springers of this noble roof are formed of solid and weighty stone; the vault which they support is of a stalactical stone, specifically much lighter. The ribs are intersected with delicate trellis-work, thrown, says a poetical antiquary, "over the whole ceiling, like a web of embroidery." It is observable that the rosettes, here profusely distributed, are not repeated in a single instance. Over the high altar are curiously introduced, amongst the countless ornaments of this elaborate ceiling, seraphic figures, engaged in full choir on the principal musical instruments of England in the fifteenth century. On each side of the choir are thirty-one stalls, carved in oak, with rich tabernacle work, allowed to form some of the finest antient church-carving remaining in this country. The great east window is usually said to be the largest window in England. The glass occupies a space of 78 feet 10 inches, by 35 feet 6

S.W. VIEW OF GLOUCESTER

inches. Seven tiers in one division of this magnificent window still retain stained glass but in so decayed a condition that it has been aptly described as resembling, in its present state, the tissue of a carpet. The pavement before the high altar consists of painted bricks, on many of which are delineated the devices of Edward II.; the Abbot Sebroke; and the Clares and De Spencers, Earls of Gloucester. The present altar-screen is a neat, and not inappropriate, erection of stone, raised under the direction of Dr. Luxmore, then dean of this cathedral, in the year 1807.

The Choir is surrounded by oratories and passages, in the Anglo-Norman style of architecture.

Over the aisle which surrounds the choir is a gallery, connecting the upper aisles, which has the property of transmitting sound along its walls in an extraordinary degree, and is popularly known by the name of The Whispering Gallery. It is not easy to determine from what principle this curious property is derived; but it has been observed that "the thinness of the walls, and the suspension of the gallery, as it were, in the air, may tend to render it sonorous." The masonry, though good, is not remarkably smooth. The gallery is 75 feet long; about 3 feet broad; and 8 feet high; and forms half an ellipsis.

The Lady's Chapel was built between the years 1457 and 1498, and is replete with architectural and monumental grandeur and interest. When this building was designed, minuteness and delicacy of decoration, in pointed architecture, were carried to their highest degree of perfection. The whole fabric may be termed a lovely lanthorn of perforated stone-work, originally filled with painted glass. A comparatively modern and discrepant altar piece of stucco has been removed, and the remains of the antient altar are now disclosed. They consist of tabernacle work, richly ornamented, and covered with thick coats of paint, in various bold colours; but the whole has been shamefully mutilated by the tasteless and bigoted reformers of past ages.

Nearly every part of the cathedral abounds in sepulchral or cenotaphial monuments. The most superb and curious of these is the *monument of King Edward II.* whose remains were removed to this place from Berkeley Castle. This tomb is situated near the high altar, and is enriched with the recumbent figure of the deceased king, finely carved and in excellent preservation. King Edward III. shortly after he had mounted the throne, visited this tomb, with much show of filial reverence, and attended by his whole court. It then became the pious fashion to make pilgrimages hither; and it should be constantly borne in mind, as a very curious and memorable fact, whilst we contemplate this cathedral, that nearly the whole of the church, beyond the nave, was rebuilt, in its present costly manner, by the aid of oblations made in these reverential visits.

The South Transept presents vestiges of Norman architecture, blended with the lighter graces of the pointed style, in the manner of the fourteenth century. The North Transept is wholly of the latter date. Underneath the church is a Crypt, supposed to have formed part of a fabric founded by Aldred, Archbishop of York, and completed in 1058, but shortly afterwards destroyed, in its principal divisions, by fire. In this crypt, or undercroft, are the remains of several chapels. On the north side of the cathedral are The Cloisters, which were begun by Abbot Horton, in 1351, and completed by Abbot Frowcester, in 1390. These constitute the best-preserved and most beautiful example of cloisters now remaining in England. Each side of the square is about 148 feet in length. The sides and roofs are richly and delicately worked. The windows are, at present, glazed in the common way; but, when filled with painted glass, must have contributed a lustrous magnificence to these ambulatories, most exalting to the imagination.

The Parochial Churches are six in number, and are, in several instances, of a respectable architectural character. The *Church of St. Mary de Crypt* is, perhaps, entitled to the first attention of the examiner. This is a handsome, cruciform, building of stone, with a tower of considerable altitude, rising from the centre. The architecture is chiefly in the pointed style of the fourteenth century, but, in the western front are still some remains of a fabric constructed by Bishop Chichester, about 1137. The interior contains several well-executed and interesting monuments. Adjoining the church is a free grammar school; founded, in 1528, by John Coke, alderman of Gloucester. The *Church of St. Michael* is a commodious structure, also of stone. The pointed style prevails throughout, but not with elegance of effect, except as regards the tower, which is a well-proportioned erection, tastefully ornamented, and appears to have been built in the early part of the fifteenth century. The *Church of St. Nicholas*, situated on the north side of the Westgate Street, is, at present, entered by a descent of several steps. From the west end rises a handsome tower, surmounted by a spire, now truncated. This abridgement in height took place a few years back, in consequence of decay. The building presents examples of many architectural styles, but is by no means eminent for beauty. The *Church of St Mary de Lode* adjoins the precincts of the cathedral, towards the west. This building will appear of little interest, to any other than the examiner with whom antiquity is admitted as a satisfactory substitute for elegance of design, and neatness of preservation. The interior is, however, deserving of attentive investigation, as it affords considerable remains of Anglo-Norman architecture. In the chancel is an antient monumental figure, absurdly said to be that of King Lucius. The *Church of St. John the Baptist* is a modern stone building, with the exception of the steeple, which is probably of the fourteenth century. The modern building was finished in 1734, and is of a common-place character. *St. Aldate's Church* is a small and unornamented fabric, composed of brick, erected about the year 1750.

The Shire Hall is a spacious and ornamental structure, erected after the designs of Mr. Smirke, and composed of stone from the quarries of Bath and Leckhampton. The principal front is 82 feet in length, and the building is 300 feet in depth. The chief entrance is by a portico of the Ionic order, having four columns, 32 feet in height. The two courts are of a semicircular form, and nearly of the same dimensions; 70 feet by 46; and 33 feet in height.

The Tolsey, or Tolbooth, occupying the angle of the south and west streets, is a respectable building, erected on the site of an antient fabric having the same denomination, shortly after the year 1749. Over the pediment, in front, are placed the city arms. The quarter sessions are held on the ground-floor, and above is the Council-chamber, a commodious apartment, in which is transacted the ordinary business of the city and corporation. In this room are portraits of his Royal Highness the Duke of Gloucester, and the late Duke of Norfolk.

Before the erection of the hall noticed above, the assizes and quarter sessions were held in a building still existing, termed the Booth Hall. This is situated behind an inn of that name, and is a rude fabric of timber frame-work, built in the reign of Elizabeth.

The County Gaol is situated on the border of the river Severn, and on the site of the antient *Castle of Gloucester*, which fortress was erected shortly subsequent to the Norman Conquest. After experiencing many vicissitudes, memorable in national history, the keep of the castle was long used as a gaol for the county: but it proved both inconvenient and insecure, as a prison; and a new structure was, accordingly, erected upon its site, and was completed for the reception of prisoners in 1791. The new gaol was planned and built under the direction of the late Sir George Onesiphorus Paul, Bart. a gentleman whose public exertions for the benefit of several institutions in this county, will be long remembered with gratitude and veneration. Attached to the gaol is a *Bridewell*. The regulations, for the management of both prisons, are founded on exemplary principles of good sense and benevolence.

The CITY GAOL, situated at the bottom of Southgate Street, was built about the year 1782, but on a scale unhappily too limited for its destined purpose. A considerable augmentation has been recently effected, and the tread-wheel is very judiciously introduced for the employment of offenders.

Pre-eminent among the CHARITABLE FOUNDATIONS of Gloucester is the INFIRMARY, which was built by voluntary subscription, "at the suggestion, and under the auspices of, the late Lord Botetourt, and the Hon. and Rev. Dr. Talbot." We are happy to add, in the words of the account whence we have extracted the foregoing passage, that those humane persons lived to see this monument of their benevolence "completed, and amply supported." The building which is spacious and appropriate, was aided by a grant from the crown of 9,200 feet of timber, and was opened in the year 1755. The medical gentlemen connected with this institution, attend gratuitously. The total amount of annual subscriptions for the year ending Dec. 31, 1823, was £1628. 10s. 6d.

The HOUSE OF INDUSTRY was established in the year 1703, as an asylum for the destitute, and a school of wholesome discipline for paupers who had fallen into habits of idleness and profligacy. The institution is supported by rates levied for that purpose, and the management is vested in a corporation, under the title of the governor, deputy-governor, and guardian of the poor, of the city of Gloucester.

ST. BARTHOLOMEW'S HOSPITAL was founded by William Myparty, in the reign of Henry II. but was first endowed with an efficient revenue through the liberality of King Henry III. The original constitution was that of a society of religious persons, consisting of a master and five priests, with 32 poor people. After the dissolution of religious houses, the whole property of this hospital was granted, by letters patent of Queen Elizabeth, to the mayor and burgesses, for the maintenance of a minister, a physician, a surgeon, and 40 poor people. About the year 1789, the buildings were re-edified, in a very appropriate manner, attention being paid in the design to the architectural style which prevailed in the sixteenth century. The revenues now maintain a master and 58 pensioners, each of whom has a separate chamber, and a small plot of garden ground. We feel it a duty to observe, that this is one of the most satisfactory asylums of its description that we have inspected.

The LUNATIC ASYLUM is a spacious building, erected on an eligible spot, by private contribution.

Among the most useful institutions, lately promoted by the judicious exercise of a benevolent disposition, must be noticed the MAGDALEN ASYLUM, situated in St. Mary's Square, and supported by voluntary subscription.

The INSTITUTIONS FOR GRATUITOUS EDUCATION are highly honourable to the liberality of the inhabitants, in past ages as well as at the present time. We have already noticed, as a foundation of a superior kind, the grammar-school of St. Mary de Crypt.

The BLUE COAT HOSPITAL was founded in pursuance of the will of Sir Thomas Rich, Bart. of Sunning, county of Berks, A.D. 1666, for the education and maintenance of 20 poor boys, on the plan of the Hospital of Christ Church, in London, and also for the apprenticing of six boys annually. The building has been lately re-edified, in a commodious and appropriate manner.

A handsome building, desirably situated, was opened in 1817, as a NATIONAL SCHOOL; and the establishment is supported by donations and voluntary contributions.

To the honour of this city, SUNDAY SCHOOLS were here first instituted, at the suggestion of the late ROBERT RAIKES, Esq. Every parish in Gloucester maintains a school of this kind; and there is, also, an establishment termed the GLOUCESTER POOR SCHOOL, which is chiefly supported from funds humanely bequeathed by two individuals.

The NEW BRIDGE over the Severn, a view of which is given in our engraving representing the city from a north-westerly point of observation, is a plain but substantial structure, of one arch, 87 feet in span, composed of stone, and executed after the designs, and under the direction of Mr. Smirke.

The Severn is a river of inconsiderable width at Gloucester, and divides into two channels, about one mile above the town, enclosing the tract called the Isle of Alney, at the southern extremity of which those branches again unite. The river is subject to floods, and is difficult of navigation between this port and Bristol. Brigs, sloops, and trows, are the largest vessels which now reach so high as Gloucester; and the trade of the port is, in consequence, prejudicially restricted. This has been long a subject of particular regret, as the geographical situation of the city is, certainly, calculated to render it a port of great utility and profit, for the distribution of various articles through the midland districts. To obviate the inconveniences proceeding from the dangerous and uncertain navigation of the river between Gloucester, Bristol, South Wales, and the Forest of Dean, a CANAL, intended to open a communication between this port and the Severn, near Berkeley, was begun in 1794; and, after an interruption, chiefly caused by public circumstances of an unfavourable character, has been resumed, and is now approaching towards completion. Great local advantages may, assuredly, be expected; and we are firmly of opinion that the day on which the whole of this undertaking shall be brought to a successful conclusion, will be the most important in all the varied history of the capital of Gloucestershire.

The Gloucester and Berkeley Canal is from 70 to 90 feet wide, and 18 feet deep; and, when finished, may be navigated with safety by the largest West Indiamen. There are two basins constructed at Gloucester, for the reception of vessels; and we have considered these appendages of a port, now first rising to its due rank in the scale of British marts, to be of such distinguished and growing interest, that no work professing to present graphic illustrations of the most prominent objects in the county, could be deemed satisfactory if it left them unnoticed. Beyond the basin are seen, in the annexed view, the *Cathedral*; the *county gaol*; and adjacent domestic buildings of the city, with the steeple of St. Nicholas rising towards the west.

The contractors have undertaken to complete the whole of the works by the 1st day of October, 1825; and it is calculated that the entire expense of the canal and basins will amount to about £420,000. The Quay is fairly commodious; and the old Custom-house, which is a small and humble building, is now forsaken for a more capacious fabric in St. Mary's Square. A rail-road leads from the basin to the town of Cheltenham.

In the immediate vicinity of the city, upon the south-east, is a SALINE APERIENT AND CHALYBEATE SPA, of increasing reputation. The springs were accidentally discovered in the year 1814. In a local publication it is observed that "the water, when freshly drawn from the pump, is clear and sparkling; emits a sulphurous smell; and has a salt, or brackish, taste. It exudes through a thick stratum of blue clay, which is diffused through a great part of the vale of Gloucester." It is ascertained, by analysis, "that the impregnations, on which the virtues of saline chalybeate waters depend, are more abundant in the Gloucester water than in any hitherto observed in this country." The buildings are extensive, and annually increasing. The *Pump Room* is 40 feet in length, by 26 feet in width, and is a handsome and agreeable apartment, with adjacent hot and cold baths. The attached grounds, which are about seven acres in extent, are laid out with much correctness of taste. The centre is verdant, and a broad terrace walk, planted with umbrageous trees, conducts round the whole of the grounds, and forms a pleasing promenade.

The dwellings constructed at this spa, for the reception of the invalid or fashionable visiter, are commodious, genteel, and desirable. An air of elegant tranquillity prevails in this retreat; and we are sanctioned by the growing opinion of the public, in thinking that few places, celebrated for mineral waters, are more congenial than the Spa of Gloucester to the wishes of those who are suffering under disease, or are desirous of the moderate enjoyment of gay and inspiriting, but select, society.

BADMINTON

2

Badminton House

THE ducal mansion of Badminton ranks, in many points of view, amongst the finest and most estimable seats of Great Britain. In amplitude of dimensions and splendour of architectural embellishment, this residence is, indeed, well calculated for a noble family of the highest consideration, with an establishment suited to stately habits and the exercise of a dignified hospitality. It may, however, be contended that a design more strictly classical, and legitimately grand, might have been adopted in a pile of such magnificent proportions. The surrounding country, likewise, is not so conspicuous for picturesque attractions as are many parts of Gloucestershire; and the adjunct of fine scenery is, assuredly, essential to the completion of august effect in a palatial edifice. In reply to such objections it should be observed that the buildings have experienced considerable improvement, from the display of a very correct taste, in numerous progressive alterations; and it may be proudly and truly said that a structure, far inferior in architectural character, could not fail of being deemed worthy the occupancy of a prince, whilst its apartments were so munificently adorned with works of art as are those of Badminton.

This noble seat is situated in the south-eastern part of Gloucestershire, at the distance of about twenty-six miles from the city of Gloucester, ten from Tetbury, and eight from Chipping Sodbury.

At the time of the Norman survey Badminton was the property of Ernulfus de Hesding. The name is written *Madmintune* in the record termed Domesday, and the estate is there said to be situated in the hundred of *Grimboldeston*. In the reign of Henry III. this manor became the property of the Boteler family, previously seated in Warwickshire, who assumed the name of Boteler from the official situation of their ancestor, Radulphus Pincerna, butler to Robert Earl of Mellent and Leicester, in the time of King Henry I. This family flourished at Badminton between three and four centuries, in the course of which long term of residence many of its representatives received the honour of knighthood, and several filled the office of High Sheriff of the county of Gloucester. But, except as to the trust reposed in them through that official dignity, little is now known of the Botelers of Badminton more than that they "fought and hunted," and married and left heirs, to continue the name, and to repeat the same round of avocations and enjoyments. Nor does any monumental relic assist, at the present day, in perpetuating the common-place records of their house, except that there is still to be seen, in the church attached to the mansion of Badminton, a slab of grey stone, having an inlay of brass, on which are engraved the figures of two knights, with a lion rampant in a scutcheon. Round the edge are the following remains of inscription: *Radulphus Botiler, Miles dominus.*

Nicholas, the last proprietor of the name of Boteler, sold this manor, in 1608, to Thomas Somerset, third son of Edward, Earl of Worcester, afterwards created Viscount Cashel, in the Irish peerage. Elizabeth, the only daughter of that nobleman, dying unmarried, bequeathed the estate of Badminton to Henry Somerset, Lord Herbert, who succeeded to the honours of his father, the Marquess of Worcester, and was, in the year 1682, created Duke of Beaufort. This illustrious family derives its descent from Henry-Beaufort, third Duke of Somerset, great grandson of John of Gaunt, Duke of Lancaster. His Grace Henry-Charles Somerset, Duke of Beaufort, K.G. &c. &c. the present possessor of this domain, is sixth in descent from the first peer advanced to the ducal coronet of Beaufort.

Raglan, or Ragland Castle, in Monmouthshire, the antient residence of the Somerset family, having been dismantled by order of Parliament, after the gallant and memorable defence of that fortress against Fairfax by the Marquess of Worcester, Henry, the first Duke of Beaufort, erected the present mansion of Badminton, partly on the site of the decayed manor-house of the Botelers. Some curious particulars, concerning the arrangement of the large household of this nobleman, are contained in the "Life of Francis North, Baron of Guilford," written by Roger North; and as these anecdotes are not only topographically connected with the place now under notice, but present a pleasing and valuable picture of the simplicity and good taste with which the rites of hospitality were sometimes performed in years towards the close of the 17th century, the insertion of a few extracts in the present page must be appropriate and desirable.

It is stated, in the work named above, that the Lord Chief Justice North, afterwards Lord Keeper Guilford, "concluding his circuit at Bristol, made a visit at Badminton to the Duke of Beaufort, and staid about a week. The Duke," observes our author, "had above 2000*l. per annum* in his hands, which he managed by stewards, bailiffs, and servants. The husbandmen, &c. were of his family, and provided for in his large expanded house. He had about two hundred persons in his family, all provided for; and in his capital house nine original tables covered every day. For the accommodation of so many, a large hall was built, with a sort of alcove at one end, for distinction; but yet the whole lay in view of him that was chief, who had power to do what was proper for keeping order amongst them; and it was his charge to see it done. All the provisions of the family came from foreign parts, as merchandize; soap and candle were made in the house; so, likewise, the malt was ground there, and all the drink that came to the Duke's table was made of malt, dried on the leads of his house. Those are large, and the lanthorn is in the centre of an asterisk.

"Glades are cut through the wood of all the country round, four or five in a quarter, almost *à perte de vue*. Divers of the gentlemen cut their trees and hedges to humour his vistas, and some planted their hills in his lines, for compliment at their own charge. At the entrance where coaches ordinarily came in, the Duke built a neat dwelling-house, but pompous stables, which would accommodate forty horses. This was called the inn, and was contrived for the ease of the suitors, as I may call them; for, instead of half a crown to his servants at calling horse, sixpence there, for form, served the turn; and no servant of his came near a gentleman's horse, but they were brought by their own servants, except such as lodged, whose equipages were in his own stables.

"As for the Duke and Duchess and their friends, there was no time of the day without diversion. Breakfast in her gallery, which opened into the gardens, and parks with the several sorts of deer to be visited; and, if required, mounting-horses of the Duke's were brought for all the company. And so in the afternoon, when the ladies were disposed to air, and the gentlemen with them, coaches and six came to hold them all.

"At half an hour after eleven the bell rang to prayers; the same at six in the evening.

"The ordinary pastime of the ladies was in a gallery, where the Duchess had divers gentlewomen commonly at work on embroidery and fringe-making; for all the beds of state were made and furnished in the house. The meals were very neat, but not gross; no servants attended but those called gentlemen. The table was an oblong, and not an oval; and the Duchess with two daughters only sat at the upper end. If the gentlemen chose a glass of wine, civil offers were made either to go down into the vaults, which were very long and sumptuous, or the servants, at a sign given, attended with salvers, &c. and many a brisk round went about; but no sitting at table *with tobacco and healths*, as the too-common use is. This way of entertaining continued a week while we were there, with incomparable variety, for the Duke had always some new project in building, walling, or planting, which he would shew, and ask his friends' advice about. Nothing was forced or strained, but easy and familiar, as if it was (and really so I thought it to be) the common course and way of living in that family."[1]

Henry, first Duke of Beaufort, who thus blended the strictest temperance and economy with a noble hospitality, and preserved so amiable a simplicity of habits in the midst of a princely establishment, was deservedly high in the confidence of King Charles II. by whom he was constituted Lord Lieutenant of Gloucestershire, Lord President of the Council in Wales, and Lord Lieutenant of the county and city of Bristol. His Grace inherited the undeviating loyalty which had characterised his celebrated grandfather, the defender of Raglan Castle, but he was doomed to exercise this hereditary virtue when loyalty itself was, unhappily, no longer compatible with the best interests of the common weal. He exerted himself at Bristol in opposition to the Duke of Monmouth; and, at a still more threatening period, endeavoured to secure that city for the weak and erring James, when the great majority of the nation had decided in favour of the Prince of Orange. Declining to take the oaths to William, on his elevation to the throne, the Duke passed the remainder of life in retirement, chiefly at Badminton, where he found amusement in perfecting the buildings and plantations of the stately seat which has since constituted the principal country residence of his descendants.

BADMINTON HOUSE is a very extensive fabric of stone. A French model was adopted in the design of this building, as was too frequently the practice with English architects, in years towards the commencement of the 18th century, without a due consideration of the difference of climate and manners in the two countries. The formal paved court and jet d'eau have long since been removed, and considerable architectural alterations, the whole of which are improvements, have been effected in the exterior of the mansion. The principal front consists of a grand central elevation, with wings and spacious pavilions. The architectural embellishments of the great central compartment are of the Corinthian order, and in the tympanum of the angular pediment are placed the family arms, of large proportions, and sculptured in stone. The East, or Garden front, is also richly ornamented, and constitutes a beautiful, as well as superb, façade. We present views of both these elevations, from which it will be perceived that the building, in its present state, is of a character vast, sumptuous and commanding.

From the eastern and western divisions rise octangular turrets, each having a cupola surmounted by a vane. The back and west side are unornamented.

The INTERIOR of this noble mansion is extremely magnificent. The chief suite of rooms is, indeed, of princely splendour, and the whole of the apartments are enriched with numerous paintings, many of which cannot fail of affording high gratification to the connoisseur. In the following enumeration of the rooms usually shown to visiters, we notice such of the pictures as appear to be of leading interest.

The HALL is 52 feet long; 27 feet 4 inches wide; and 27 feet 4 inches in height. The sides and door-cases are ornamented with good carving, and the ceiling is finely stuccoed. The paintings are by *Wootton*, who was honoured with the particular patronage of the third Duke of Beaufort, and consist chiefly of representations of favourite horses and field sports, with some incidental portraits.

The most distinguished persons introduced are Henry, third Duke of Beaufort; Lord Charles Noel Somerset, his brother; Sir Watkin Williams Wynne; and George-Henry, Earl of Litchfield. Here is also preserved a large and curious sarcophagus, composed of one block of marble. The sculpture represents, in alto relievo, a grand bacchanalian procession. This valuable antique was dug from some ruins at Rome, and presented to Henry, third Duke of Beaufort, by Cardinal Alberoni. Whilst noticing this Duke, in connexion with a work of art, it may be observed that many of the pictures now at Badminton were collected by him, during his travels in Italy.

The NORTH BREAKFAST ROOM contains several paintings by Wootton, in the best manner of that artist. The subjects are chiefly horses and dogs, but some family portraits are introduced.

Amongst the most attractive pictures in the SOUTH BREAKFAST ROOM will be observed,

Jesus at Simon's House, by Bassan.
St. Anthony preaching to the Fish, by G. Poussin.
An old Glassman with Matches, by Canavagio.
Two Landscapes, by Wootton.

The EAST BREAKFAST ROOM contains, among other works of art,

Two perspective Ruins, by Viviani.
A Battle-piece, by Parocelle.
Winter-scene, by Vandermeer.
Landscape, by De Heush.
A View of Tintern Abbey, by Arnold.
Two Landscapes, by Swaneveldt.

The chimney-piece of this apartment is delicately executed by Brookshaw, after a painting by Angelica Kauffman, representing the *Return of Telemachus* and his *Reception by Penelope*.

The DINING ROOM is an elegant apartment, 43 feet in length; 23 feet 6 inches in width; and 15 feet in height. The chimney-piece, and ornamental compartments of the door-cases, are enriched with exquisite carvings by Grinling Gibbons, representing fish, fruit, flowers, and foliage. Over the fire-place is a three-quarter portrait of *Elizabeth, Lady Herbert*, daughter of Sir William Dormer, Knt. by Vandyck. In other parts of the room are the following whole-length portraits of Dukes and Duchesses of Beaufort:

Henry, 1st Duke. Sir Godfrey Kneller.
Mary, 1st Duchess. Dahl.
Henry, 2nd Duke. Hudson.
Rachel, Duchess of Beaufort. The same.
Charles Noel, 4th Duke. The same.
Elizabeth, 4th Duchess. Gainsborough.

The DRAWING-ROOM is a superb apartment, erected by the present Duke, under the direction of Jeffrey Wyattville, Esq. architect. The dimensions of this noble room are 50 feet in length, 34 in width, and 20 in height. The hangings and curtains are crimson; and, pendant from the ceiling, are two beautiful lustres of cut glass, each having sockets for twenty-five lights. Placed on a platform of black marble, in a recess built for the purpose, at the upper end of the room, is a splendid and unique cabinet, very large and lofty, inlaid, in compartments with marble of various tints, representing birds and flowers. At the top is a clock, surmounted by the family arms, carved and gilt. It may be observed that the assemblage of gorgeous curiosities at Fonthill was deemed incomplete, since this rare and beautiful cabinet was unattainable to the collector.

But the Drawing-room of Badminton House has more potent claims on the admiration of the examiner, than those which proceed from sumptuous furniture, and mere cabinet-work, however beautiful in execution and splendid in effect. The PAINTINGS here reposited are, in many instances, of inestimable excellence. The following demand particular notice:

Two large and beautiful pieces by Claude Lorraine. The subjects (incidental to much exquisite scenery) are *The Temptation*, and *Christ and his Disciples at Emmaus.*

Four highly-finished and excellent pictures by Guido, each representing an *Evangelist.*

The above named six pictures are, certainly, the finest in the Badminton collection, and rank among the best specimens of their respective masters.

A curious *Allegorical Painting* by Salvator Rosa, representing the different European sovereigns as various animals, among which occur the hog, the fox, the wolf, the sheep, the cow, and the ass. Over the last-mentioned animal is thrown the pontifical pall; and the sightless goddess Fortune is depicted as showering her gifts on the whole undeserving group. In consequence of this satirical effusion Salvator was banished from Rome.

A Holy Family, by J. Romano.
Two fine Architectural Subjects. Ghisolphi.
A Battle-piece. Borgognone.
A Landscape. Wyck.
Bacchus and Cupid. Cignani.

The LIBRARY is a very fine room, of the following dimensions: 47 feet in length, exclusive of the book-cases; 23 feet in width; and 20 feet in height. This apartment was built by the present duke, at the same time with the Drawing-room, and both open into a conservatory, through which is obtained a good view of the adjacent park scenery. The collection of books is extensive and valuable. Ranged above the book-shelves, on each side of the room, is a curious and valuable series of portraits, representing the chief personages of the Beaufort family, from John of Gaunt, their ancestor, to the present time. Many of these were brought hither from Raglan Castle, and it is often said that the whole are originals, but the critical inquirer will be inclined to doubt the correctness of this assertion, as regards those which refer to very early periods.

The whole are well-executed, and several are highly interesting. The succession is as follows:

John of Gaunt, 4th son of King Edward III.
John de Beaufort, eldest son of John of Gaunt, created Earl of Somerset, 1396.
Edmond de Beaufort, Earl of Mortein, in Normandy, created Marquess of Dorset, 21st of Henry VI.
Henry de Beaufort, son of the preceding nobleman, who, in his father's life, became Duke of Somerset, and K.G.
Charles Somerset, only son of Henry Duke of Somerset, created Earl of Worcester, 5th of Hen. VIII.
Sir Henry Somerset, 2nd Earl of Worcester, ob. 1549.
William Somerset, 3rd Earl of Worcester, K.G.

Edward Somerset, 4th Earl of Worcester, K.G. Master of the horse to Q. Elizabeth, and Lord Privy Seal, temp. James I. Ob. 1627-8.

Henry Somerset, 1st Marquess of Worcester. The loyal and celebrated defender of Raglan Castle.

Edward, 2nd Marquess of Worcester. Author of "A Century of the Names and Scantlings of such Inventions," &c. Ob. 1667.

Henry, 1st Duke of Beaufort, by Sir Peter Lely.

Henry, 2nd Duke.

Henry, 3rd Duke.

Charles-Noel, 4th Duke.

Henry, 5th Duke.

Henry-Charles, 6th and present Duke, K.G., by Phillips.

Among several portraits in the DUKE'S DRESSING ROOM, the following require notice:

Queen Elizabeth, by Zucchero.
Family of the 1st Duke of Beaufort.
James, Duke of Ormonde.
Lord Capel.

In the DUCHESS'S DRESSING ROOM are some Landscapes, a Battle-piece, and other pictures, by Wootton. In the same apartment are, likewise,

A Portrait of himself by A. Caracci; a *Battle-piece* by Borgognone; and several other good pictures.

The BILLIARD ROOM is 32 feet in length; 20 in width; and 13 feet 6 inches in height. In this room are the following, among other valuable paintings:

Erasmus, a very curious portrait by Holbein. The expression of countenance acute and argumentative, sceptical and querulous, yet elegant.

Sir Thomas More, the equally curious companion to the above, by Holbein. The harsh lineaments of the countenance express strength of mind and great penetration, but in every line may be read a rigid inflexibility of disposition.

The *Doge Grimani,* and his brother the *Cardinal Tintoretti.*

Charles I. by Vandyck.

Landscapes by Bolognese, Caracci, Bassan, Berghem, Polemberg, and Poussin.

The ANTE ROOM, situated between the Billiard and Drawing Rooms, contains very numerous cabinet and other pictures. The following attract particular observation:

Holy Family. Raphael.

Head of himself, by Guido; an exquisite portrait.

Two excellent pictures by Teniers; the subjects *St. Anthony's Temptation*, and *Boors drinking.*

Jesus and the Woman of Samaria. Annibal Caracci.

Church of Redemption at Venice. Canaletti.
Madona and Bambino. Guercino.
Holy Family, Lionardi da Vinci.
Joseph's Flight into Egypt. Carlo Maratti.
Head of the Virgin Mary. The same.
Angel's Head in the Annunciation. The same.
Diana and Actæon. The same.
Venus in the Sea. The same.

The CHAPEL, a spacious building which adjoins the mansion on the south-east, acts as the parochial church of Badminton, and was re-edified by the late Duke, about the year 1785. This structure is destitute of architectural ornament on the exterior, but internally is designed and adorned with great elegance and simplicity. The aisles are divided by taper pillars, and the ceiling of each aisle is coved, and enriched with delicate stucco-work. The pavement of the recess for the communion-table is of Florentine Mosaic, displaying the family arms in large proportions. The steps are of jasper and verd antique; and over the table is a painting of *Our Saviour disputing in the Temple*, by G. Ghetzi. In the tribune is the lower part of a Cartoon, by Raphael, the subject of which is the *Transfiguration.*

In different parts of the church are several monuments of the Beaufort family. To the north of the Altar is a monument erected to the memory of Henry, second Duke; Lady Rachel Noel, his second wife; and Henry Somerset, their eldest son, who succeeded as third Duke of Beaufort. To the south of the same sacred spot is the monument of Charles Noel Somerset, fourth Duke. Both the above named monuments have full-length effigies of the deceased, by *Rysbrach*, which are remarkable for energy of expression, and have, in many respects, great merit, but are deficient in that impressive and solemn simplicity which constitutes the most estimable characteristic of monumental sculpture.

The mansion stands towards the centre of an imparked demesne, enclosed by a wall nearly nine miles in extent. In our extract from the account of this seat by Roger North, is a notice of the "lines" of wood, and "vistas," planted and formed by the first Duke. These avenues still, in a great part, remain in their original forms, and the forest-trees of which they are composed are, in many instances, of a noble growth. From the print of Badminton inserted in the History of Gloucestershire by Sir Robert Atkyns, it will be seen that the home-demesne was then disfigured by an immense labyrinth, and vast plantations of box, yew, and other evergreens, disposed in various fantastic shapes. Those monstrous creations no longer exist, as evidences of the perverted taste of the age in which they were considered as beauties; and in every recent alteration the "genius of the place" has been duly consulted, and its dictates acted upon. The imparked lands possess little variety of surface, and are deficient in ornamental water, but their amplitude of extent, and the noble diversity of radiating avenues by which they are intersected, render them worthy appendages to one of the finest seats in the midland counties. The grand approach to the house is through the park from WORCESTER LODGE, a lofty and handsome stone building, forming a dignified entrance to the domain. The distance between this lodge and the mansion is about two miles and three quarters.

1. Life of Francis North, Baron of Guilford, &c. pp.132-4.

DODINGTON PARK

3

Dodington Park

THIS fine domain is situated at a short distance from Badminton, towards the south-west.

The earliest written materials for a history of Dodington must be sought in the usual repository of antient manorial intelligence, the Book of Domesday. But the occupation of this place and its vicinity by the Romans, is proved by various tangible traces of those august conquerors. To the north-east of Dodington, and situated partly in the parish of Little Sodbury and partly in that of Old Sodbury, are the remains of a camp, bearing decisive marks of having been formed by the Romans, although it was, probably, occupied in after-times by other contending powers. This castrametation is placed on a commanding eminence, and is in a state of preservation truly gratifying to the antiquary. The area in which it stands contains rather more than 30 acres. Its form is that of an oblong, with the angles rounded off. Towards the west the ground sinks precipitously, and forms a natural defence, aided, however, by a ditch, which extends about half the length of the camp. On other sides it is protected by a double vallum and ditch. The inner vallum is nearly 20 feet in height, and its ditch ten feet in depth and width. The outer vallum is of inferior altitude, but its ditch is wider and deeper than that on the inner side. It may be observed that iron bullets, in considerable numbers, are frequently turned up by the plough in the adjoining field.—This is the last work in a line of five camps, which are seated on points of the Cotswold Hills, between Painswick and Little Sodbury.

Leland notices a "yerthen pott, with Romayne coynes, found in Dodington Felde", and "Pottles, exceeding finely nely'd, and florished in the Romanes tymes, digged out of the ground," in the same field. He also states that "a glasse, with bones, yn a sepulchre, was found by Dodington Church, on the heighway."

Connected with the subject of remote antiquities, it may be remarked that there are, within the bounds of Dodington park, several tumuli, the contents of which have not been examined. On digging in their vicinity, about the year 1800, four human skeletons were found. The antient church, mentioned by Leland, was little more than two furlongs distant from these barrows.

The manor of Dodington belonged, at the time of the Norman Survey, to the family of Berkeley of Dursley, and appears to have constituted a place of their residence, for it is said in the Testa de Nevill that "the *Lady of Dudinton*, who *was* wife of Henry de Berkeley, is to be married, and her land is worth £8." The male line of this branch of the Berkeleys ended in the person of Nicholas de Berkeley, who died in 1382; and Maud, his sister and heir, carried the estate, by marriage, to Robert de Cantelupe. Elizabeth, their only daughter and heir, was married to Richard Chedder, but the male line again failing, Dodington devolved by descent to the family of Wekys, or Wickes, of whom the earliest mention, in regard to this manor, occurs in the 13th year of King Edward IV. By the Wekys family the estate was enjoyed until the time of Queen Elizabeth; early in whose reign it was sold, by Robert Wekys, to Giles Codrington, Esq. with whose descendants it has ever since remained.

The antient and highly respectable family of Codrington was seated, from a very early period, on an estate contiguous to Dodington, bearing their own name. The whole parish of Codrington, forming a property of singular beauty, was in their possession for many ages, but passed from them, for a short time, by virtue of a marriage, to the Bampfyldes of Somersetshire. The present baronet has, however, lately recovered it by purchase, and has thus obtained the estimable opportunity of adding the property of his ancestors to his other extensive possessions. It is worthy of remark that Sir Robert Atkyns, and after him the other historians of Gloucestershire, describe Giles Codrington, the original purchaser of Dodington, as having descended "from Robert Codrington, of the Didmarton family;" whereas Didmarton did not pass by marriage to the family of Codrington, until some years after they had settled at the place now under notice.

We regret that our limits prevent us from offering more than a few brief observations, respecting several distinguished members of this antient family.

Sir John De Codrington, Knt. was standard-bearer to Henry V. and for his good services in the wars in France under that king, received the honour of knighthood. He attained the advanced age of 111 years, and dying, in 1475, on his patrimonial estate, was buried in the church of Codrington.

Robert Codrington, styled by Sir R. Atkyns "a younger brother of this family," and author of "several ingenious treatises;" attracted considerable notice as writer of the Life and Death of Robert Devereux, the ill-fated Earl of Essex.

General Christopher Codrington, born at Barbadoes in the year 1668, will be long remembered with veneration, for the munificence of his charitable bequests, and the liberality of his benefaction to All Souls' College, Oxford, of which Society he had been a fellow. General Codrington was one of the most accomplished scholars and gentlemen of his age. He was for some time captain-general, and governor in chief, of all the Leeward and Caribbee islands, but devoted his declining years to retirement and study. He died at Barbadoes on the 7th of April, 1711; but his remains were brought to England, and buried in the Chapel of All Souls' College. By his last will he bequeathed two plantations in Barbadoes, and other West Indian property, to the Society for the Propagation of the Gospel in Foreign Parts. On the College of which he had been fellow, and of which his name and acquirements are a just and honourable boast, he bestowed his collection of books, the pecuniary value of which was estimated at £6,000 and also the sum of ten thousand pounds, for the purpose of erecting a library. The building constructed by means of this splendid benefaction, is one of the finest rooms of its kind in the kingdom, and is adorned with a statue of its amiable and public-spirited founder.

The title of Baronet was granted to the family of Codrington, of Dodington Park, in the year 1721.

It is said by Sir Robert Atkyns that the mansion of Dodington, as standing in the early part of the 18th century, and which remained until recent years, was erected by Robert Wekys, in the time of Queen Mary, or early in that of her successor: but Leland, writing in the reign of Henry VIII. mentions the house of Bodington as having been *then* newly built, and observes that "part of Drisilege (Dursly) Castle was brought," to assist in forming this structure. It is traditionally said that Queen Elizabeth honoured this seat with a visit. It would, likewise, appear that a more antient house was then standing, in the immediate contiguity of the modern pile. "The olde place of Dodington," says the topographer last named, is "withyn the mote, by the new."

All traces of the antient buildings are now supplanted by a superb mansion, commenced in the year 1797, and successfully completed after the designs, and under the direction, of the late James Wyatt, Esq. This structure occupies nearly the same site as the former house, and is one of the finest efforts in domestic, or rather palatial, architecture of the tasteful artist from whose plans it was erected. Mr. Wyatt was here fortunate in working upon a site eminent for beauty; and his exertions were also favoured by a circumstance impressively stated by Vitruvius to be essential to the felicitous completion of an architect's views, and the full display of his merits; namely, a correct judgment in the proprietor of the domain.

This mansion is of noble proportions, and, whether beheld as a splendid whole, or examined in the detail of its component parts, is a grand and most attractive example of Grecian architecture. The principal front, which is sustained in its magnificence by contiguous park-scenery indescribably rich, is conspicuous for the union of dignified elegance with attic simplicity. On investigating the parts which produce this unmixed beauty of general effect, it will be found that the finely-symmetrical portico is, perhaps, without a parallel in modern exhibitions of the grace and harmony resulting from combinations formed on the principles of classical architecture.

The interior is marked throughout by blended elegance and comfort, and affords an exemplary specimen of that delicate taste, and sound judgment, in appropriating the various divisions of a mansion to the wants and style of life suited to its owner, for which the late James Wyatt was more celebrated than any other architect of his era. The grand suite of apartments commands admiration for convenience of arrangement, beauty of proportions, and a judicious disposition of ornamental particulars unusually magnificent. The Entrance Hall is a noble apartment, and the richly-decorated ceiling of this room may be pronounced a triumph of modern art, as regards this species of architectural embellishment. The principal staircase is one of the finest that we have seen. If less superb it would, indeed, constitute a blamable discrepancy, and be unworthy of conducting to ranges of apartments so splendid.

A mansion, thus classical and dignified in character, would still be deficient in genial embellishment, if it failed to afford examples of pictorial excellence. It may be truly said that no deficiency, or neglected point of tasteful enrichment, is here observable. The collection of paintings is extensive, and contains many estimable works of Claude Lorraine, Rembrandt, Rubens, Teniers, Carlo Dolce, Cuyp, Vandervelde, Cornelius Janssen, Andrea del Sarto, Wouvermans, and other celebrated masters. Among these, perhaps, the following are the most striking:

Holy Family. And. del Sarto.
Simeon, Anna, and the child Jesus. Rembrandt.
Family Portraits. Father, Mother, and daughter. Cornelius Janssen.
Presentation in the Temple. Philip de Champagne.
Our Saviour crowned with Thorns. Carlo Dolce.
Madonna and Child. Guido Reni.
St. John. Guercino.
St. Jerome. Guido.
St. Francis. The same.
Our Saviour in his Jewish Robes. Rembrandt.
A Sea-Piece. Wm. Vandervelde.
A Storm at Sea. Molyn.
Reapers. Teniers.
Horseman, Cattle, and Dogs. Cuyp.
Hunted Stag. Pynaker.
Interior of a Cathedral. Steenwyck.

View of Venice. Canaletti.
Portrait of Mrs. Porter. Sir Joshua Reynolds.

This picture is curious, as having laid the foundation of Sir Joshua's fame as a portrait-painter. Mrs. Porter is here represented in the dress which she wore when she took leave of the stage. Having accidentally fractured her leg before she made her farewell speech, she was brought forward sitting in a chair, and in that attitude she is represented on the canvass.

It may not be superfluous to observe that the mansion of Dodington is brilliantly lighted with oil gas, and was nearly the first private establishment in England at which this mode of lighting was adopted.

The Park of Dodington contains nearly 700 acres, and is about five miles in circumference. In our account of Badminton we have suggested that the country, in the vicinity of these seats, is by no means conspicuous for natural charms. The power of contrast is seldom more forcibly exhibited than to the traveller who quits the uninteresting adjacent country, and enters the domain of Dodington. This lovely territory would, indeed, seem to stand by itself, quite unconnected with the surrounding scenery. The surface is beautifully varied by hill and dale, whilst wood and water, the indispensable requisites of the picturesque, combine with every home-view, in a delightful abundance. Springs of lucid water are numerous in this fine tract; and from those known by the name of "The Seven Springs" the river Frome derives its origin. This river is inconsequential throughout the distant parts of its course, but its channel is here artificially enlarged, and its lovely waters flow through the park, with a breadth and amplitude due to the noble genius of the place. The plantations are very extensive, and are disposed with eminent correctness of taste.

We must not quit a spot where there is so much to admire, without observing that the CHURCH of Dodington, which adjoins the house, is a fine example of Grecian architecture, erected at the same time with the mansion. The porch is supported by columns of the Doric order. The form of the church is that of the Grecian cross, and the fabric is surmounted by a dome. The interior is highly, though chastely, ornamented, and the attention of the spectator is impressively attracted by the solid beauty of the pillars, which spring from the four angles of the cross, and apparently support the dome. Each pillar is a single block of Bath free-stone, seventeen feet in height and two feet six inches in diameter. The recent date of this structure forbids us to look within its walls for circumstances of monumental interest; and we shall be joined by very numerous voices in the hope that it will be long before its classic embellishments receive additions so mournful. The remote ancestry of the respected proprietor of this domain were interred in the neighbouring church of Codrington; but we have already adverted to the most curious inscription in that place of sepulture, which is to the memory of Sir John de Codrington, standard-bearer to Henry V. during his wars in France.

4

Spring Park

THE SEAT OF THE RIGHT HONOURABLE
THOMAS-REYNOLDS MORETON, LORD DUCIE

THE country on the borders of the river Frome, or Stroud, is in many parts, enchantingly picturesque. Hills, verdant, lofty, and graceful, rise in long succession, forming, with the Cotswolds, a part of that central chain of billowy elevations, which proceeds, with some interruption, and many fluctuations in altitude, from Derbyshire towards the Land's-end, Cornwall, or south-western extremity of Great Britain. In addition to the waters of the Frome, this part of Gloucestershire is intersected by numerous rivulets, that fertilize the soft dingles through which they flow, and blend with lawn and wood, in a perpetual variety of agreeable landscapes. Beech is the natural growth of the hills; but the advantage of the frequent streams has led to the introduction of an important branch of manufacture, beneath whose influence the woods have, in a great measure, fallen, except where preserved for ornament; and in their place has risen a scene of busy cultivation, which has not destructively interfered with the charms of nature, and may be said merely to have imparted to them a new and unusual colouring. The town of Stroud, near which is situated the seat we are about to describe, is in the centre of the CLOTHING DISTRICT; and the reader, not acquainted with this part of Gloucestershire, cannot readily form just ideas respecting the extent, or character, of the effect produced on the face of the country by the operations of a trade so vast, and which employs so large a population.

We shall embrace the more appropriate opportunity of a future article for some remarks on this manufacture, and the district over which it spreads; but must here observe that the hilly and beautiful borders of the river, in the vicinity of Stroud, are animated, throughout, by works and buildings connected with this great trade in its different branches. The watery lowlands, or bottoms, as they are locally denominated, present one continuous display of well-organized industry; and the rising lands, even to the summit of the boldest elevations, are enriched with the mansions of capitalists engaged in manufacture, or dotted with the white cottages of subordinate actors in the busy scene. The vales which open between the hills, on both sides of the principal stream, vary in character between the softness of the smiling glen and the stern, but romantic, cast of the broad and devious ravine. By one of the finest of these interstices in the hilly tract, we approach the mansion and demesne of Spring Park.

Here, as we proceed, all gradually subsides into tranquillity, and the passenger becomes unavoidably subject to an emotion of surprise at the profound quiet which prevails, in so close a proximity to the bustle of manufacture and commerce. Beyond the boundaries of the park, every acre is a little world, no particle or drop of which appears to be unvalued or unused. On entering this demesne, the power of contrast is exhibited with peculiar strength. When we behold hill after hill, throughout several miles of country, devoted to the growth of ornamental wood; and large sheets of water in the vale, free from the steam of manufacture, and left to the naiads and wild fowl, whilst their banks are browsed by the lordly deer, grown confident in experiencing the

Spring Park

security of his solitude; we become sensible, in a very unusual degree, to impressions of baronial grandeur, and the dignity of elevated seclusion.

Spring Park is situated in the parish of Woodchester, at the distance of about five miles from the town of Stroud, and two miles from the village of Stanley St. Leonard. The character of scenery in this extensive park is not much varied, but is romantic, fine, and highly picturesque. A lovely vale, several miles in length, of devious progress, and no great width, constitutes the principal feature in the domain. A stream, which formerly glided within narrow limits, is now artificially enlarged, and is seen from all the chief rides and avenues; in some places assuming the breadth and character of a river, in others shut into basins, and shewing the fashion of ages in which the Catholic families of old preferred a well-stocked fishery, however inelegant in outline, to all the graces of a meandering but unprofitable flow of decorative water. The hills by which this vale is closely encompassed, rise in a beautiful variety of shape and position:—locking into each other; crossing at sharp angles; or melting in a graceful wavy outline, with most picturesque felicity of vicissitude.

The house is situated in the vale, towards the centre of the park, and is screened, in every direction, by hills richly covered with wood. It is of moderate height, as best becomes a country mansion; and is a square fabric, composed of stone, enclosing a court, and shewing three fronts. The principal entrance is by a light and pleasing portico, of the Ionic order; and in the vicinity of the garden-front is a handsome conservatory. The interior has lately been much improved, and enlarged with new Library, Breakfast-parlour, and Dining-room, under the direction of Mr. J. Adey Repton, architect.

In the principal apartments are some pictures, of various degrees of interest, including several family portraits. Amongst the latter is an original of Sir Robert Ducie, Bart. a citizen of London, by means of whose commercial industry and success, the fortunes of this antient family were renovated in the 17th century. The Ducie family traces its origin to the Ducies of Normandy; their ancestor having entered England in aid of Isabel, consort of Edward II. From that period, until the reign of the eighth Henry, they enjoyed large estates in Staffordshire, and there maintained their principal seat. But the hereditary property was greatly injured, in the time of King Henry VIII. by James Ducie, Esq. whose grandson, the above-named Sir Robert, entered into commercial speculations at London, for which city he served the office of Lord Mayor. He was banker to King Charles I. and, although he lost £80,000 by the account of his royal master, amassed a great fortune for the benefit of his descendants. Sir William Ducie, Bart. his second son, was created Viscount Down, in the peerage of Ireland, by King Charles II. and Matthew Ducie-Morton, great nephew of the first Lord Down, was advanced, in the year 1720, to the dignity of an English peer, by the title of Lord Ducie, baron of Tortworth, county of Gloucester.

This noble family had its chief residence, for several ages, at Tortworth, distant about four miles from the town of Berkeley; the mansion at which place is now dilapidated, and in the occupation of a farmer.

The estate of Spring Park, together with the manor of Woodchester, was possessed by the family of Maltravers in the reign of Edward I. with which family it remained until the time of Richard II. in whose reign Eleanor, sister and heiress of Henry Maltravers, carried this estate by marriage to John, second son of Richard Earl of Arundel. The property continued with the Earls of Arundel through several successions, but was possessed by the crown, early in the reign of Elizabeth, by which sovereign it was granted to George and John Huntley. Of the Huntley family it was purchased by Sir Robert Ducie, Bart. the refounder of the antient house of Ducie, whose great and merited success as a merchant and banker we have already noticed.

The parish of Woodchester has acquired much interest with the antiquary, and with men of cultivated taste in general, from the discovery of various splendid Roman remains, consisting chiefly of the vestiges of a Roman villa, of great magnitude, which evidently constituted the residence of a person of high distinction. These noble remains are situated in, and near, the parochial church-yard; and have been minutely described by the late Mr. Lysons, in a work illustrated with many plates of tesselated pavements, and fragments of sculpture and architecture.

5

Gatcombe Park

THE SEAT OF DAVID RICARDO, ESQ.

THIS domain is situated in the parishes of Avening and Hampton, at the distance of about three miles from the town of Tetbury, towards the north. The surrounding country partakes of the hilly, varied, and picturesque character which we have noticed in our account of Spring Park. The Roman colonists of Britain, who had a warm sensibility to the beauties of nature, and evinced an exquisite taste in selecting the sites of their summer villæ, well knew the charms of this district, and erected in it many superb dwellings, remains of which, as particularly in the instance of Woodchester, have occasionally been discovered; and more will, probably, be found, in distant days, for the gratification of future antiquaries. Few inland tracts, indeed, afford more felicitous combinations of the points essential to a judicious choice in the ground-plot of a family-mansion, if we except, perhaps, the inroads on nature and quiet effected by the wide spread of the clothing manufacture, which will scarcely be viewed as desirable circumstances of neighbouring arrangement, to those who are not connected with that great branch of national industry. A country fertile of hills, various in altitude, and folding into each other, often with a rich woody clothing, admits of numerous vales, or bottoms, which, without an injurious limitation of prospects, confer upon an ornamented domain an idea of *entirety* of territory, highly favourable to its dignity of aspect. This advantage, among other beneficial circumstances more seriously desirable, is, in some degree, possessed by the mansion of the Ricardo family, which is placed on the ascent of a narrow valley, bounded by high beech wood, with intermingled oak and ash, on one side, whilst the rising ground, in an opposite direction, is decorated with clumps, and other efforts of the landscape-gardener. The house looks down on a spacious and fine lawn; which terminates in waters, expanded by the hand of art to an ornamental breadth of surface.

This manor is mentioned in the book of Domesday as part of the property of the crown, and was given by William the Conqueror to the monastery of Caen, in Normandy, from which foundation it passed, at the dissolution of alien priories, to the nuns of Sion, in Middlesex. King Henry VIII. granted it to Andrews, Lord Windsor, in exchange for Stanwell, in the county last named; and Thomas Lord Windsor sold the property to Samuel Sheppard, Esq. whose family resided at an antient seat, termed Hampton Park. It may be remarked that this former residence of the Sheppards is still standing, and has experienced few alterations, except the insertion of sash windows. It is situated near the church of Minching-Hampton, and an engraved view of the building, in its original state, is given in the history of Gloucestershire by Sir R. Atkyns.

Of Philip Sheppard, Esq. the estate of Gatcombe was purchased about the year 1814, by the late David Ricardo, Esq, M.P. for the Irish borough of Portarlington. This gentleman, well known for his senatorial labours, and as a writer on political economy, passed in the dignified retirement of Gatcombe those parts of his declining years in which he relaxed from numerous important avocations, and here breathed his last, at the age of 60, in September 1823. He was

GATCOMBE PARK

succeeded, in this part of his extensive possessions, by his son, David Ricardo, Esq, by whom the mansion and grounds are maintained in the same excellent state of preservation as in the time of his late able, persevering, and patriotic father.

The present elegant house was built by Edward Sheppard, Esq, father of the gentleman who sold this estate to Mr. Ricardo. It is a well-proportioned and spacious mansion, handsome on the exterior, and internally well designed and arranged. The chief portico of entrance is highly ornamental to the fabric; and the fine and very extensive conservatory, which adjoins one end of the house, and runs in a line with the principal front, is chastely planned and delicately executed. The best apartments of the mansion are enriched with a few pleasing pictures, among which must be noticed a good landscape, by N. Berchem.

The subject of another of these paintings will scarcely fail to bring to the spectator's recollection the calculating habits of the late eminent and lamented proprietor of the domain, and his ingenious inquiries in political conomy. The action of this piece illustrates the parable of the Master of the Vineyard, and his labourers, hired in different parts of the day, but all paid alike. The time chosen is that in which the master says, "Friend! I do thee no wrong: did I not agree with thee for a penny?"

The attached grounds are extremely beautiful. Their principal features, as we have already suggested, consist of a narrow and velvetty vale, the lofty barriers of which are lined with hanging woods, chiefly of beech. The water, which we have before noticed, is distant about one mile from the house, and covers not less than fifteen acres. At the rear of the mansion a road winds along the vale, having at its commencement a handsome lodge, situated upon the high road from Minching-Hampton to Tetbury.

In the vicinity of Gatcombe are several tumuli, or barrows. Within the park is a tall and upright single stone, erected, probably, in commemoration of some striking event, once deemed of great importance, but now forgotten. It is thought that these vestiges bear reference to some unchronicled battles of the Saxons and Danes, between whom several sanguinary conflicts certainly took place in this part of Gloucestershire. Rudder was informed that an "old sword" was dug from one of the tumuli, about the year 1750; and Mr. Rudge records the circumstance of two antient rings having been found near a monumental single stone at Gatcombe.

REDLAND COURT

6

Redland Court

THE SEAT OF SIR RICHARD VAUGHAN

REDLAND is a hamlet to the extensive parish of Westbury-upon-Trim, and derives its principal ornament from the very respectable seat of which we present an engraved view. The hamlet of Redland is distant from Bristol little more than one mile, towards the north-west; and when we observe that the country in this direction abounds in natural charms, it will be readily supposed that so favoured a tract, in the immediate vicinity of a great commercial city, is less conspicuous for rural simplicity than for richness of cultivation, and plenitude of architectural embellishment. The environs of Bristol will form the subjects of several future articles, and we shall now merely observe, in general terms, that they comprise, in a fascinating quickness of alternation, some of the boldest and softest beauties of South Britain. The windings of the river Avon, and those fine eminences on its shores, in the vicinage of Clifton; the distant grand flow of the Severn; a natural inequality of surface; and expanses of wood, merely pruned of exuberance by the arborist, and retaining their native luxuriance and freedom of plant; are some of the charms which render the north-western environs of Bristol superlatively attractive to the visitor, and have gained them renown in "prose and rhyme."

The villas, and houses of various denominations, raised in so desirable a district, are very numerous, and have rapidly increased in recent years. It has been remarked, by an ingenious contemporary, that an antient mansion, of sedate and consistent architectural character, in the vicinity of the frivolous and ill-placed buildings of modern date, too frequently seen in the neighbourhood of large cities, may be regarded as a venerable and old-fashioned English gentleman, amongst a vast assemblage of spruce and affected fops. This just comparison does not hold good, with a severity of application, in the present instance. Within the limits of Westbury are many truly estimable mansions; but the idea of antient gentility, as opposed to the flimsiness of modern fashion, is enforced on the mind when we view the grave outlines, and handsome, but somewhat formal and weighty, decorations of Redland Court, in the neighbourhood of many non-descript erections, which are so unlike anything an architect could have devised, that they would literally appear to have been "made" by some builder's "journey men."

The hamlet of Redland is situated in the tithing of *Stoke Bishop*, so called from the circumstance of it's having, at one time, belonged to the bishops of Constance, in Normandy, and afterwards to the bishops of Worcester. This hamlet formed a part of the possessions of the Abbey of Tewkesbury. It is shewn by Sir R. Atkyns that the privileges of a court-leet, with waifs and felons' goods in this domain, were allowed to that foundation, in a writ of *Quo Warranto* brought against the abbot and brothers, in the 15th of Edward I. After the dissolution of monastic houses, this property was obtained by the family of Wilson. Egion Wilson and Dorothy his wife, and Miles Wilson, joined in levying a fine of the manor of *Rydland*, otherwise *Th' Ridland*, to John Foxton, in the sixth of Edward VI. It was subsequently vested, for many years, in the

Cossins family; from whom it passed to John Innys, Esq. brother of Mr. Innys, a bookseller, who made a celebrated, and perhaps matchless, collection of maps, and views, in nearly 100 volumes. Redland was afterwards possessed by the nephew of Mr. Innys, Jeremy Baker, Esq. who died about the year 1798. The estate was then sold to Henry Seymour, Esq. at whose decease it was purchased, of his son, by the present proprietor, Sir Richard Vaughan.

The mansion was erected by John Cossins, Esq. about the year 1730. It is placed on elevated ground, near the high road from Westbury to Bristol, and is a spacious and handsome building, having many extrinsic ornaments which respect for a past age renders venerable, and in some degree pleasing, as the memorials of antient courtliness of manners and dignity of family bearing. The front is enriched with Ionic columns, and the principal door-way is approached by a wide flight of steps. The interior presents many large, and some well-proportioned, apartments. Considerable alterations in the building were made by Mr. Baker, but much of the fitting-up of this mansion still exhibits the best specimen we have seen, of the ornaments and arrangements of the dwelling of a private gentleman in the first half of the 18th century. The gardens and their appendages have desirably been stripped of much of their original formality, by the improving hands of the former proprietor, Mr. Seymour, and the present possessor of this seat of dignified comfort, Sir Richard Vaughan. Ameliorated by modern taste, they still retain sufficient of their original character for the purpose of a due *keeping* with the solid, ornamented, and, in some degree, stately building to which they are attached.

As the parochial church is at a considerable distance from the hamlet of Redland, Mr. Cossins, the founder of Redland Court, erected a Chapel near his mansion, in the year 1740, and endowed it with lands for the support of a minister. He also built a parsonage-house, at the expense of £1000. The chapel is a handsome structure of freestone, entered at the west end by a portico, having four columns of the Ionic order. A single bell hangs under a cupola of considerable elegance. The interior is designed and furnished with conspicuous delicacy of taste. The recess for the altar is of a semi-octangular form, carved in compartments, and ornamented with a painting of the embalming of Christ. The communion-table is of marble, and is supported by a gilt eagle. Before it two other eagles are raised on pedestals, for the support of books. In a small vestry-room, to the south of the entrance, is a handsome monument, erected to the memory of several persons of the family of Cossins, or allied to it by marriage. Among the persons enumerated is John Cossins, Esq. (builder of Redland Court, and of this chapel) who died April 19th, 1759, at the age of 77. Here are also busts, by Rysbrach, of the same John Cossins, Esq. and Mrs. Martha Cossins, his wife, daughter of Andrew Innys, of Bristol, gent.

7

Cirencester

THIS market and borough town, on the south-east border of Gloucestershire, is situated on the River Churn, and is distant 17 miles from the city of Gloucester, and 36 from Bristol. It covers a considerable tract of ground, and consists of eleven streets, the whole of which, however, are irregular in plan and buildings, and one only, according to modern notions, is sufficiently wide for the purposes of beauty, traffic, and free ventilation. The great majority of the houses are *old,* rather than *antient*; very few evincing an earlier date of construction than the medium years of the 17th century. They are chiefly whitened, or coloured yellow; a practice that prevails in many parts of the neighbouring Cotswold district, and is frequently ornamental to the green uplands and watered dales of this picturesque county. The dwellings of the principal inhabitants are spacious and detached, with the advantage of large plots of garden-ground. On the borders of the town, in several directions, some handsome houses have been recently erected. The place wears a cheerful, rather than a busy aspect; no peculiar manufacture, or branch of commerce, being here cultivated on a large scale.

Cirencester was a place of importance at the earliest date, concerning which we possess historical information, and constituted the capital of the British tribe, or nation, termed the Dobuni. In the 12th Iter of Antoninus it is mentioned under the name of *Duro-Cornovium,* which is supposed to be a corrupt reading of the proper appellation, as it is termed by Ptolemy and Ravennas *Duro-Corinium.* The celebrated monk, Richard of Cirencester, after noticing several cities of the Dobuni, observes that " the most venerable of all was *Corinium,*" which he states to have been "a famous city."

In several pages of the present work we have opportunities of showing that this part of Gloucestershire contained numerous villas, and other dwellings, of the Romans, in addition to regular military stations. it appears, indeed, to have been thickly inhabited by that people, and the town under notice was not only fortified by them as a strong hold, but was selected as a favourite place of residence and visit. A recent ingenious historian (the Rev. T. D. Fosbroke) maintains "that Cirencester was," as regards this district, "the great metropolis of the Romans, or resort of pleasure and amusement; while Gloucester, and the hills about the Severn, were the chief military positions, the last named city, on account of the river, having peculiar advantages with respect to commerce." It is said by the monk Richard to have been one of the ten cities placed under the *Latian law,* or allowed the same privileges as were granted to the antient inhabitants of Latium.

A consideration of its brilliant fortunes while under the dominion of the Romans, and the numerous vestiges discovered of that polished people, spread a potent charm over this town, in the esteem of the antiquary, and, indeed, in that of every man of taste and feeling. It is approached by bold, high, and, in many places, well-preserved, Roman roads; while the

CIRENCESTER CHURCH

frequent discoveries made, on almost every new removal of soil, denote the widely-spread wrecks of power and splendour hidden from the eye by comparatively modern buildings, and other accumulations on the surface of this antient "Chester" of the conquerors of Britain. It might, indeed, be figuratively termed the skeleton of a Roman station.

The walls of Cirencester were more than two miles in extent, and were evidently constructed by the Romans, as Leland mentions, on the authority of the abbot of this place, that Roman inscriptions were seen upon many of the stones. The only letters recollected, however, were those which follow; Pont Max. Not any part of the antient walls is now remaining, above ground; but considerable traces of foundation exist on the east and on the south sides. We are informed by Rudder that a small part was uncovered, in the year 1774, when it was ascertained that the wall had been eight feet in thickness, and strongly cemented with lime, sand, and gravel.

A tract of land, termed the *Leauses*, situated on the south-east side of the town, and now comprised in the grounds attached to the seat of the Master family, has yielded a rich harvest of Roman antiquities, in many different ages, from the time of Leland down to the present date. Dr. Stukeley supposes the Roman Prætorium to have stood here; but this is mere antiquarian conjecture. Carved and inscribed stones; tessellated pavements; coins; rings; intaglios; and fragments of Roman pottery, have been found in the Leauses at various times, but the most important discovery was that of a Hypocaust, which took place about 1683. Little attention, however, was bestowed on this curious relic until the year 1780, at which time the remains were explored with some care. Two sides had been destroyed, previous to the last-named date of investigation; but the building, from what remained, would appear to have been of considerable extent. This subterraneous fabric, with places for fires, and funnels for the passage of heated air, did not differ, in any curious particular, from hypocausts of the Romans discovered in other parts of Britain.

Leland, writing in the time of Henry VIII., observes that the Abbot of Cirencester told him he had seen, in the ruins of the town-walls, arched stones, engraven with large Roman letters; and Dr. Stukeley records that several lettered stones have more recently been found at Cirencester; but we believe that no account has been preserved of any other than the two following Roman inscriptions discovered at this place.

At the distance of half a mile from the town, and on a spot called the *Querns*, upon the south side of the road to Tetbury, was found a stone, bearing this funeral memorial:

D. M.
IVLIAE CASTAE.
CONIVGI VIX
ANN XXXIII

About half a century back, there was dug up, at Watermore common, just without the wall, on the south side of the town, a monumental stone, together with an urn containing bones and ashes. The stone was thus inscribed:

D. M.
P VICANAE
P VITALIS
CONIVX

Urns, and other particulars of funeral deposit, have been very frequently found, at short distances from the line of the former walls of the town, in several directions, but particularly on the south side.

Tessellated pavements, which had formed the ornamental floorings of Roman houses, have also been discovered in great abundance. These have been found in so many different parts of the present town, as well as in the Leauses, and other places in its vicinity, that it is evident the Corinium of the Romans was a city of great extent and population.

One of these was found in 1777, on digging a cellar beneath a warehouse in Dyer Street. It lay about six feet below the surface of the street, and the plaistered walls of the room to which it belonged were still remaining. They appeared to have been painted, but the figures were so far decayed that no ideas could be formed of the subjects represented. In the same street is still to be seen part of a mosaic, or tessellated, pavement, discovered in 1783, at the depth of rather more than six feet from the surface. The site is enclosed in the residence of Mrs. Selfe, relict of the late W. Selfe, Esq.; and strangers are very politely allowed to inspect this curious vestige.

In addition to the printed memorials of such discoveries, we are enabled to mention the following recent circumstances, which, if not of any striking importance, are still worth placing on record.—On digging for gravel in the garden of an attorney, whose premises are divided by a very few houses from those of the lady mentioned above, a pavement was found in the year 1824. But the object of the attorney being gravel and not antiquities, he dug up this relic of the tasteful Romans, and the soil by which it was covered, with equal indifference. In the latter part of the same year a second tessellated pavement was, fortunately, revealed to a more refined and judicious proprietor. On making some alterations for the enlargement of a house occupied by a steward of Earl Bathurst, a pavement was found, of square proportions, having two concentric circles in the ornamented parts. In the centre is the figure of Orpheus, surrounded by various animals. It unavoidably sustained much injury from the work-people, as a large tree was growing over the centre of the pavement, and had insinuated its roots between many of the tesseræ.

Whilst noticing traces of the Romans in this neighbourhood, it may be proper to observe that there is, on the south-west side of the town, an earth-work, of an elliptical form, locally known by the name of the *Bull Ring*, but which was, probably, a Roman amphitheatre. The area is in dimensions about sixty-three yards by forty-six, and is enclosed by mounds of earth, about twenty feet in height, having rows of seats formed from the earth on their sides. It has two entrances, one on the east and the other in an opposite direction. There is, also, a subterranean approach from the south, which conducts between two stone walls, the passage being about two feet six inches wide.

When the Romans finally quitted this island, the government of Cirencester reverted to the Britons. But the hands of our British forefathers were enfeebled by party divisions, and the possession of this antient metropolis was wrested from them, in the year 577, by the West Saxons, under Cealwin and Cuthwin, immediately after the decisive battle at *Dyrham*, near Chipping Sodbury, some particulars of which are given in our notice of that place.

This was, from an early period, a walled town of considerable strength, and was provided with a castle, which stood on its south-west side. The date at which the castle of Cirencester was erected is not known. It was garrisoned by Robert, Earl of Gloucester, in the cause of the Empress Maud; but was surprised and reduced by King Stephen. In the reign of Henry III. it was maintained, in opposition to the government, by the refractory barons; a circumstance productive of its downfall, for, on the royal party gaining an ascendancy, the king issued a warrant for the demolition of this fortress, and it was razed to the ground.

Although deprived of its protecting castle, Cirencester continued to be esteemed a strong hold, for many ages in which a capability of defence constituted the principal inducement for the visits of distinguished persons. King John assembled here a large army, when he drew the sword against a discontented nobility and an oppressed people, in the sixteenth year of his reign; and in 1322, Edward II. held within the embattled walls of this town the revelry of Christmas, at which time he collected round him the friends of his crown and person, to deliberate on measures for opposing the confederacy of the Earl of Lancaster and the Lords of the Marches, against the court favourite, Hugh le Despencer. The result of their counsels was the concentration of the royal forces at this place. But fate, in these hours, pressed heavily on the footsteps of the devoted king, and the gaudy tragedy of his life soon after closed in Berkeley castle.

Cirencester attained some notoriety, from the suppression, by its citizens, of the rebellion raised against Henry IV. by the Duke of Surrey, the Earls of Rutland, Salisbury, Gloucester, and other noblemen. On the detection of this conspiracy, and the consequent advance of the royal army, several of the insurgent chiefs retreated, with their forces, to Cirencester. The troops encamped without the walls, and the chiefs took quarters in the town. The mayor, perceiving a want of military vigilance in the rebel army, assembled 400 men in the night, and attacked the noblemen in their quarters. The Duke of Surrey and Earl of Salisbury fled to the abbey for shelter, but were there seized and beheaded, with scarcely "shriving time allowed." The Duke of Exeter and the Earl of Gloucester escaped, by the tops of houses, to their camp; but found it abandoned by the panic-stricken soldiers, who had dispersed on bearing noises of contention in the town. In reward of this loyal service, King Henry, with characteristical frugality, granted to the inhabitants all the property of the conspirators found in the town—except plate, jewels, and money. He also bestowed on them an annual present of venison and wine.

In our account of Gloucester we had occasion to mention the exemplary courage shown by the females of that city, on an emergency of importance. We have the pleasing opportunity of again noticing the zeal and intrepidity evinced by the ladies of Gloucestershire, in times of old. King Henry, in his largess of venison to regale the citizens, and wine to drink to the royal health, gives to the men *four does* and one hogshead of wine. He likewise grants to the women, "who as well as the men had performed unto him good service," *six bucks*, and (more, we must suppose, than would be wanted for their share of the annual banquets) another hogshead of wine.

In the civil wars of the seventeenth century the inhabitants sided with the parliament, and the place was strongly garrisoned, under the command of Colonel Fettiplace. We are told, in a pamphlet of that time, that the town was then esteemed "the key of Gloucestershire." It is, writes this author, "strong in its natural situation, being about half way round encompassed with water, a great part with a high wall, and the remainder secured by strong works." All these favourable circumstances were, however, insufficient for its preservation. On the 21st of January, 1642, Prince Rupert advanced towards the town, and an assault commenced on the 2nd of February. The garrison displayed much courage, but the king's troops succeeded in gaining possession of the town, with a trifling loss. On the part of the besieged 300 were killed, 160 wounded, and 1200 taken prisoners. The town was afterwards alternately possessed by both parties, but was not again regularly garrisoned and defended in the cause of either.—Several curious publications of the time, relating to the above siege, are reprinted in Part the second of *Bibliotheca Gloucestrensis*.

An *Abbey* was founded at Cirencester by King Henry I. which flourished until the general dissolution of monastic establishments, in the reign of Henry VIII.; at which time the buildings were taken down, and the materials dispersed, by order of that tasteless and tyrannical sovereign.

CIRENCESTER

With such implicit attention was his command obeyed, that the precise site of the once rich and beautiful abbey cannot now be ascertained. The structure stood, unquestionably, on the north side of the parochial church. The site it occupied, and the adjacent lands, after several changes in proprietors, have been for many ages vested in the family of Masters, who have a mansion on the Abbey-lands, with extensive attached pleasure-grounds. This residence forms the subject of an engraving in the present work; and some few further particulars concerning the dissolved abbey, may, perhaps, be best introduced in the descriptive pages which accompany that engraved view.

Cirencester formerly contained three *parochial churches*, one of which alone remains in use at the present time. This is dedicated to St. John the Evangelist, and has been justly ranked amongst the most magnificent parochial edifices in the kingdom. It is extremely to be regretted that a structure so truly beautiful, should occupy a site unfavourable to its display. Domestic buildings, generally of a mean character, crowd round its base, and, in many instances, lean for support against its enriched walls. Front the principal streets, parts only, of the extensive and symmetrical pile, are open to view; and thus, in regard to the exterior, is the design of the builder, who was, as his work evinces, and as was usual with the artists of the middle ages, an enthusiast in the picturesque of architecture, injuriously defeated.

Although a view completely pleasing be unattainable, it may be desirable to notice the most advantageous positions for an inspection of this edifice, as a pictorial object. From the Abbey-gardens its northern side, graceful tower, and clustering pinnacles, are beheld, in captivating splendour. An east view (by no means the most interesting point of observation) is obtained from the attached burial-yard. The most striking perspective exhibition of the fabric is presented at various parts of the park, and grounds, appertaining to the mansion of Earl Bathurst. But these latter views are singular and curious, rather than satisfactorily picturesque.

The Church of Cirencester is uniformly in the pointed style of the fifteenth century; an era in which the ecclesiastical architecture of England was ennobled by a plenitude, without a meretricious redundance, of decoration. It was completed only a few years before the suppression of the Abbey, but an adherence to one consistent design is visible throughout the whole of its principal parts. The tower, which rises from the west end to the height of 134 feet, is of just proportions, and copiously ornamented with statues and pinnacles. Mr. Bigland observes that it "was certainly built before 1416, as the arms of France (over the great window) is several *fleur de lis*, which was last used by Henry IV." The nave was completed in the time of the last abbot, who submitted to the king's supremacy in 1534.

On the outside of the church, beneath the parapet, on the north wall of the nave, are some pieces of sculpture, curious from the subject rather than the style in which they are executed. These represent a series of figures, having various musical instruments used in the fifteenth century, and are designed for the characters of a *Whitsun Ale*. The lord of the revel wears a cap and feather, and holds a scroll on which is the following inscription

BE MERRIE

It is observed by Rudder that festivals of the above description are still common in some villages in this part of Gloucestershire. The Whitsun Ale, as still practised, adds that writer, "is a burlesque representation of the state of a great man and his family, in antient times. The *Dramatis Personae* are the lord; his lady; the steward; sword-bearer; mace-bearer; musician; and fool, with other servants occasionally. The scene is the lord's ball, which is commonly a barn; and near it a may-pole is erected on the occasion."

Under the parapet, on the south side, is another series of sculptured figures, supposed to represent some of the characters in the old Mysteries, or Moralities. These pieces of sculpture are best inspected from the leads, over the aisles.

On the south side of the church is a beautiful porch, 38 feet in length, and 50 feet in height. The rich decorations of the exterior comprise many grotesque figures, and twelve vacant niches, in which were formerly placed statues of the Apostles. The parapet is perforated, and the ceiling adorned with fan-work, springing from slender single pillars at the sides.

The interior of the church consists of a nave, side aisles, and chancel, with five chapels. The central division is separated from the side aisles by two rows of clustered columns, five in each. Attached to the capitals are figures of cherubim, with escutcheons, and other armorial insignia of benefactors to the building. The nave is divided from the chancel by a gallery, or screen, containing a good organ; but this modern addition is lamentably destructive of the effect intended to be produced, on a view from the west end. The windows were originally filled with painted glass; but considerable mutilations having occurred, the remaining glass was taken down, a few years back, and placed in the great east and west window, under the direction of the late S. Lysons, Esq. and at the expense of two ladies, Mrs. Cripps and Mrs. Williams. The paintings chiefly represent the persons of the Trinity; various saints of the Roman Calendar; and benefactors to the windows; with some armorial devices. Among the numerous pieces collected in the west window, is a portrait, supposed to be designed for that of Richard, Duke of York, father of Edward IV. Part of the glass in the east window, representing members of the Langley family, was brought from the church of Siddington, in this neighbourhood.

In different parts of the church are some very rich *brasses*. Sepulchral decorations of this description are found in many churches of the Cotswold district of Gloucestershire, and it has been observed that "the merchants in wool, for which article this tract was long so celebrated, traded, in the fifteenth century, with the manufacturers in Flanders, where these brasses were made and given in exchange."

The *Chapels* are dedicated to Jesus; St. John; St. Catherine; St. Mary; and the Holy Trinity. In each of these buildings are monuments and sepulchral inscriptions, of various degrees of interest. The chief attention of most examiners will be attracted by those of the family of Bathurst, in Trinity Chapel. The monument of *Allen, Earl Bathurst, and his lady,* is enriched with busts of the deceased. This excellent nobleman, who died September 16th, 1775, at the age of 91, was much distinguished in the political transactions of his time, but is better known to fame, and to the affections of posterity, as a nobleman of refined taste, and the friend of Pope, Swift, Addison, and other eminent wits and elegant scholars of the ages in which he flourished. The adjacent monument of *Henry, Earl Bathurst*, Lord High Chancellor, soil of the above-mentioned Earl and Countess, has also a bust. He died on the 6th of August, 1794; and the inscription to his memory states that " his ambition was to render himself not unworthy of such parents."

Neither of the chapels demands much attention, as an architectural object, with the exception of that dedicated to St. Catherine, the ceiling of which is handsomely wrought with pendants, sculptured foliage, knots, and armorial devices. The initials J. H. for John Hakebourne, Abbot of Cirencester from 1504 to 1522; and T. R. for Thomas Ruthall, afterwards Bishop of Durham; are several times repeated; and are designed to commemorate the dignified churchmen at whose expense the roof was erected. The date, 1508, shews the time of its completion.

There are several Hospitals and Almshouses in this town, but the whole are on a small scale. Charitable donations, for the permanent benefit of the poor, have been made, in various ages, to a considerable amount, and are greatly beneficial to the indigent class of townspeople.

The *Free Grammar School* was founded, early in the sixteenth century, by Thomas Ruthall, bishop of Durham, a native of Cirencester; and was formerly a flourishing and useful establishment. The late Dr. Jenner, to whom society is indebted for the introduction of Vaccine Inoculation; the late Dr. Parry, of Bath; and the Rev. James Dallaway; received the early part of their education in this school.

Two institutions for eleemosynary instruction, receive their appellations from the colour of the dress worn by the respective children.

The *Blue School* was established, with the aid of several contributions, in 1714. The *Yellow School* was founded in pursuance of the will of Mrs. Rebecca Powell, who died in 1722, for twenty boys and the same number of girls.

The town of Cirencester constitutes a separate hundred, having received that distinction from King Henry IV., whose debt of gratitude to the inhabitants we have already noticed. It was by that king made a corporate town; but the charter was cancelled in the reign of Elizabeth. The hundred is divided into seven wards, and the steward of the manor annually appoints two high constables, and two wardsmen, or petty constables, for each ward, with other necessary officers.

This borough first acquired the permanent right of sending two burgesses to parliament, in the thirteenth year of Queen Elizabeth. The right of election lies with such inhabitants as are householders, and do not receive alms.

The manor of Cirencester was part of the antient demesnes of the crown, and is recorded as such in the book of Domesday. After various transmissions, in succeeding ages, the manorial rights, *with the hundred of Cirencester*, were purchased, in 1695, of the relict of the Earl of Newburgh, by Sir Benjamin Bathurst, ancestor of Earl Bathurst, in whom the property is now vested.

As a distinguished *Native* of this town, must be mentioned *Richard*, surnamed, from the place of his birth, *Richard of Cirencester*, an eminent scholar and antiquary of the fourteenth century. No traces have been discovered of his family, but it is ascertained that he entered into the Benedictine monastery of St. Peter, Westminster, in the year 1350. It is believed that he died in 1401, or the following year. He was author of several theological and historical works; but the performance to which he is indebted for his celebrity is the treatise entitled *De Situ Britanniæ*, containing an Itinerary, which he states to have been collected, by himself, "from some remains of records, that had been drawn up by the authority of a certain Roman general, and left by him for the use of succeeding ages." The MS. of Richard was discovered at Copenhagen, by Mr. Bertram, an English gentleman, in the year 1747, and was published by him, at the request of Dr. Stukeley. An excellent translation has recently appeared, from the pen of Mr. Hatcher, with a valuable commentary on the itinerary, by the Rev. Thomas Leman, of Bath. Mr Whitaker, in his History of Manchester, conjectures that this curious itinerary was drawn up after the year 138, and before the year 170. Mr. Hatcher observes that it is more complete in its execution than that which bears the name of Antonine, frequently correcting that document, and presenting the names of more than sixty posts and towns, before unknown.

OAKLEY PARK

8

Oakley House

THE SEAT OF THE RIGHT HONOURABLE HENRY BATHURST, EARL BATHURST, K.G. &c. &c.

AT the name of this mansion a train of pleasing associations arises in the mind. The shades of Addison, and Steele; of Pope and Swift;—of all that we have been accustomed to admire and venerate, as the brightest ornaments of early years in the eighteenth century, press on the fancy, in a glorious assemblage, and shed a lustre on the seat in which wit and worth resided with ALLEN, LORD BATHURST.

This noble and interesting residence is immediately contiguous to the town of Cirencester, and occupies the eastern extremity of a very extensive and beautiful imparked demesne.

In our account of the neighbouring town we have briefly stated the descent of the manor and hundred of Cirencester, and have there traced them, through several transmissions, to the possession of Sir Benjamin Bathurst, father of the first Earl Bathurst, by whom they were purchased in the year 1695. Allen, the first Earl, shortly after he acceded to the paternal estate, purchased of Sir Robert Atkyns, of Saperton, a large contiguous property, comprising the district termed Oakley Woods, which had formerly belonged to the Abbey of Cirencester, and afterwards, among other proprietors, to Sir John Danvers.

When these conjoined estates came into the possession of Lord Bathurst, there stood, on the site of the present mansion, a very spacious house, in the form of one half of the Roman letter H, which was built in the reign of James I. by Henry Danvers, Earl of Danby. For some time Lord Bathurst occupied, when at Cirencester, the central division; but this antient house was, at length, either wholly, or in much the greater part, taken down, and a mansion constructed under his direction, which, although apparently intended merely as an occasional residence, and not as a specimen of architecture appropriate to the beauty and extent of the attached grounds and park, was still better suited to the increasing elegance of the times, and the refinement of his habits. The house, indeed, evidently formed a secondary object of consideration, whilst his chief attention was directed to the planting and disposal of the noble parks and pleasure The consummate taste he displayed in the execution of these designs, was applauded by Pope, in the emphatical question,

> "*Who plants like Bathurst, and who builds like Boyle?*"

The mansion of Allen, Lord Bathurst, has been greatly altered, and augmented, by the late and present Earls. Though each alteration be, confessedly, an improvement, the examiner will look, with primary interest, on those parts that retain marks of days in which the wits of England's Augustan age, as regards its literature, were here assembled, round their genial friend and tasteful patron. The house in its present state is a spacious and respectable, but irregular pile. The east and west fronts are of considerable length, and the former, which looks towards the town, is a handsome elevation of freestone. We present a view of this structure as seen from the park, with the tower of the parochial church of Cirencester rising over the central compartment of the western front. From the position we have chosen, the building is, undoubtedly, seen to advantage; and it must not be concealed, that, from such a point of inspection, a flattering idea is imbibed respecting the site of the mansion. On other sides we cannot avoid perceiving that this large and interesting structure is placed much too near the town, for the attainment of real beauty and dignity of surrounding circumstances.

Several of the very numerous apartments into which the interior is divided, are large and handsome.

The ENTRANCE-HALL, together with other rooms towards the same face of the building, has been recently enlarged, after the designs of Mr. Smirke. In this apartment are a portrait of *Prior*, and a large painting, by Sir T. Lawrence, representing *Arthur, Duke of Wellington*, on horseback. The dress exactly displays that worn by his Grace at the Battle of Waterloo; and the horse is also a portrait of that which he rode, on a day so memorable in the military annals of Great Britain.

In the BREAKFAST-ROOM is a portrait of the late *Mr. Pitt*, by Romney; and the LIBRARY is ornamented with a portrait of *Alexander Pope*.

In an ANTE ROOM are delineations, in *Chiaro-scuro*, of the *Apollo Belvidere*, the *Venus de Medicis*, and the *Hercules Farnese*. On the last-named piece is inscribed G. KNELLER, AMITICÆ GRATIA. These pictures by Sir G. Kneller, when given by that artist to Pope, called forth the following verses:

> What God, what genius did the pencil move,
>   When Kneller painted these?
> 'Twas friendship, warm as Phoebus, kind as love,
>   And strong as Hercules.

These lines were not published by Pope, who was, probably, aware of their inferiority. The paintings to which they owe their origin, are, likewise, by no means admirable, as works of art, but they will be viewed as objects of curiosity and of respect, when it is recollected that they were bequeathed by Pope to his noble friend, Lord Bathurst.

The DINING ROOM is a handsome apartment, enlarged by the present Earl. It contains the following, among other portraits.

King Charles I. }
King Charles II. } Half-length, painter unknown.
Hyde, Duchess of York.
Thomas, Lord Clifford, of Chudleigh, Lord High Treasurer in the reign of Charles II.
    The initial of his name forms the first letter of the CABAL, a term well known to
    have been applied to five persons, greatly distinguished in the politics of their day;
    Clifford, Arlington, Buckingham, Ashley, and Lauderdale.
Henry Bennet, Earl of Arlington, Lord Chamberlain to Charles II. The character
    of this nobleman is more vividly depicted in the "Memoirs of the Count de
    Grammont," than are his features on the canvass of the painter.
George Villiers, Duke of Buckingham.
Henry Jermyn, Earl of St. Alban's, Steward of the Household, who is said to have
    been privately married to Queen Henrietta Maria, relict of Charles I.

John Wilmot, Earl of Rochester, a good portrait, by Henry Gascar. The countenance of this witty nobleman would appear to be indicative of better qualities than he exhibited in his brief, but most profligate, career. He is represented in a scarlet coat, a wig, and a spreading cravat, much ornamented with lace.

Barbara Villiers, Duchess of Cleveland, delineated as *Saint* Barbara! The reader may be reminded that this graceless Duchess much affected the jest of being represented in the character of the "martyr," whose christian appellation she bore. A portrait of this description she once sent to the nuns of Abbeville, but the imposition being detected, those ladies thought proper to decline receiving the proffered favour.

Louise de Querouaille, Duchess of Portsmouth.

In due association with the three portraits last named, is here seen that of *Chiffinch,* master of the revels to Charles II. His name and avocations have been rendered familiar to many persons, who would, otherwise, (not to their disadvantage), have remained ignorant of his character, by one of the novels destined to become the fashion of the day, and attributed to Sir Walter Scott. The reader, probably, will not need to be reminded that the novel to which we allude is termed Peveril of the Peak.

Over the fire-place is a line bust of *Napoleon Buonaparte.*

In the Drawing-Room is a pleasing portrait, by Hoppner, of the *present Lady Bathurst,* with one of her children in her arms.

The Billiard room is a handsome apartment, opening to the park through a modern conservatory. The following family portraits in this room will be viewed with a high degree of interest.

Allen, 1st Earl Bathurst, in his robes as a peer. On a table by his side is placed a coronet, on which his hand rests. This whole-length portrait represents the Earl in the flower of life, shortly after he was advanced to the peerage, as Baron Bathurst, in 1711. He was created Earl Bathurst in 1772.

Catherine, Countess Bathurst, wife of Allen, 1st Earl. Her ladyship was daughter of Sir Peter Apsley, of Apsley, in the county of Sussex. She died in the year 1768, in the 79th year of her age.

Henry, 2nd Earl Bathurst, Lord High Chancellor of Great Britain. His lordship was second son of Allen, the first Earl, but succeeded to the family title and estates, as his elder brother died, without issue, in 1767. Whilst the apparent heir to this earldom served his country in parliament, as representative of the county of Gloucester, or the borough of Cirencester, the younger brother applied to the study of the law, and was successively appointed solicitor-general and attorney-general to Frederick Prince of Wales. He sat in several parliaments, for the borough of Cirencester. In January, 1771, he was appointed Lord Chancellor; and in the same month was created a baron, by the title of Lord Apsley. The date of his decease, and his admirable desire of emulating the virtues of his father, as stated in the epitaph suggested by himself, we have noticed in our account of the parochial church of Cirencester.

Henry, 3rd and present Earl Bathurst, represented when a boy, and in company with his brother. A portrait of youthful elegance, simplicity, and high promise, unusually gratifying.

There is no other portrait, at Oakley, of the first Earl Bathurst, than that which we have noticed in this apartment; and it is much to be regretted that the features of a nobleman, certain of maintaining a lasting interest with posterity, were not delineated on the canvass, when an age beyond the common lot of man had increased the dignified peculiarity of his character. It is, likewise, to be wished that the representation of him had been of a more familiar kind. The Bathurst addressed by Pope, as one, who, ennobled by talent, and "unspoiled by wealth," possessed

> That secret rare, between th' extremes to move
> Of mad good-nature and of mean self-love,

would have commanded respect without the robes of peerage. We must be allowed to repeat our regret that no picture represents this tasteful and urbane nobleman, in the sparkling hilarity of a conversational hour; and to add, that surely the place best suited to such a portrait would have been the library, with representations, for its companions, of the eminent men from whose society he derived pleasure. We look at Oakley for such a tribute to an exalted display of classical refinement, and, finding it not, we feel that the mansion, however judiciously arranged, and gratifying at other points, is subject to a deficiency for which no magnificence could possibly atone.

It will not be expected that we should, in this work, enter into a regular biographical account of the former proprietor of a seat, although so distinguished and favourite a character as Allen, Lord Bathurst. But it is impossible to form a descriptive notice of the residence endeared to after-ages by the lustre of genius and the charms of benignity, without bringing to recollection the principal features in the life of him that imparts attraction to the abode.

Lord Bathurst was introduced to a knowledge of political life by his father, Sir Benjamin, and was advanced to the peerage by Queen Anne, at a period in which party-spirit raged with lamentable violence. Throughout the two succeeding reigns he persevered in conspicuous activity, but retired from public business on the accession of George III. stating his great age as the reason of his declining to accept of office. An examination of his political career would do honour to his memory; but it is from his private hours that his chief celebrity is derived. In these, whilst Walpole hunted; Chesterfield fluttered, deceiving and deceived; and Bolingbroke sullied, by licentious principles and manners, the society towards which his better genius prompted him; Lord Bathurst shone the easy and natural friend, and the constant companion, of the best scholars and the most eminent writers of his time. To name the chosen friends of his retirement, we must form a proud and gratifying list of nearly all to whom our stock of national literature is indebted for the ornaments it obtained in the first half of the eighteenth century. It may be sufficient to observe that the records of that classical æra present, as his befriended and admiring associates, Addison and Steele; Pope, Swift, Gay, and Arbuthnot; Congreve, Prior, and Rowe. In the society of these scholars and wits he passed at Oakley the happy and memorable hours of his relaxation from affairs of state, both in the early and in the mature parts of his life. Here, to those friends, and to aspirants after his favour, of all classes, he exhibited the refined taste, the sound sense, and the noble generosity, emanating from the heart but corrected by the understanding, which obtained from Pope the well-known eulogy in that poet's third epistle, or Moral Essay.

After his final relinquishment of public business, Lord Bathurst chiefly resided at this seat; and, exemplary to the last, presented to a new generation the admirable spectacle of a courtier and a wit retaining an amenity of disposition, and a vivacity of temper, until he gently sank into the grave, in the ninety-first year of his age.—If we should have a reader who is not acquainted with the following passage in a letter of Sterne to Eliza, he cannot fail of being pleased to meet with it in this work; and those who may be familiar with that romantic, but elegant, epistle, will excuse its insertion, since it affords a portraiture, peculiarly vivid, of this excellent nobleman, at a period of life in which he formed the subject of curiosity as well as veneration;—the surviving Mæcenas, strewing flowers over the ashes of the classics whom he had loved and patronised.

"Lord Bathurst," writes Sterne, "is an old friend of mine. The manner in which his notice began of me was as singular as it was polite. He came up to me one day, as I was at the Princess of Wales's court: 'I want to know you, Mr. Sterne; but it is fit you should know, also, who it is that wishes that pleasure. You have heard,' continued he, 'of an old Lord Bathurst, of whom your Popes and Swifts have sung and spoken so much. I have lived my life with geniuses of that cast, but have survived them, and, despairing ever to find their equals, it is some years since I have closed my accounts, and shut up my books, with thoughts of never opening them again. But you have kindled a desire in me of opening them once more before I die; which I now do: so go home and dine with me.' This nobleman, I say, is a prodigy; for at eighty-five he has all the wit and promptness of a man of thirty. A disposition to be pleased, and a power to please others, beyond whatever I knew: added to which a man of learning, courtesy, and feeling."

The noble demesne attached to the house of Oakley, and divided into parks, pleasure-grounds, and plantations which have long since attained the character of flourishing woods, constitutes the most important feature, in a topographical consideration of this seat. The inclosed lands devoted to ornamental purposes extend not less than four miles, from the mansion on the east, to their termination, at the road leading from Bath to Cheltenham, in a westerly direction.

This large expanse of decorated scenery was entirely designed, and laid out, by Allen, Lord Bathurst. When that nobleman acceded to the estate the only cultivated ground, immediately attached to his residence, consisted in the garden, and a few formal inclosures to the rear, or westward, of the mansion. Beyond these limited and unseemly tracts, lay the estate which he subsequently purchased of Sir R. Atkyns, then open and cheerless downs. The judicious disposal of grounds: on a large scale, was, likewise, an effort of a novel character, it must be recollected, to the lasting credit of Lord Bathurst, that he was nearly the first of those tasteful persons, who, in the early part of the last century, opposed, by the strong incitement of a better example, the disgusting formalities introduced by Le Naûtre, under the sanction of King William. In viewing this domain we must hold in remembrance, as an act of justice to the designer, that the models by which the taste of the present age is usually directed in landscape-gardening, were not then existing or devised. It has been remarked, that, previous to the very general adoption of the improvements introduced to the art of forming garden, or park, scenery, by Kent and Brown, these grounds were unrivalled, except by those at Stowe and Esher.

Whilst thus pursuing a walk of invention so little trodden, the noble designer had to combat with a variety of natural circumstances, unfavourable to the cultivation of picturesque effect. The surface of his domain, although not absolutely flat, is subject to no more than slight and graceless undulations. In water it was entirely deficient. A small lake, formed with much ingenuity and labour, is the only aquatic embellishment possessed by the grounds, in their improved state.

The domain of Oakley is formed into divisions, varied in scenery, and of different appropriation, comprising home and deer parks, and a majestic extent of woods, engrossing the whole width of the territory, and almost aspiring to the character of a forest. Numerous vistas, or rides; intersect the whole; and many picturesque *situations* have been sedulously created, several of which are provided with buildings, seats, and other circumstances of extraneous decoration.

On the northern side of the home-park is a terrace, of considerable length, accompanied, throughout the whole of its extent, by a walk of a devious, or serpentine, character, shaded by forest trees and perennial shrubs. From this umbrageous path are obtained, at numerous breaks, communications with the terrace, and agreeable views over the park, whose bosom is diversified with well-placed clumps and plantations. At the termination of the walk is a building, termed *Pope's seat*, traditionally said to have derived its name from that poet's attachment to the tranquillity and sylvan beauty which are its characteristics. A lawn expands in the front of this recluse building, and several vistas reveal striking views, having the churches of distant villages, or other strongly-marked objects, for the chief features. At the termination of the principal of these vistas, and towards the centre of the deer-park, Lord Bathurst erected, on a lofty column, a colossal statue of his royal mistress, Queen Anne.

To the west of the imparked district noticed above, is a finely-planted tract, termed the Lodge-park, beyond which are Oakley Woods, constituting the pride of this demesne. These noble woods are now in a full vigour of growth, and are intersected by numerous rides, ten of which concentrate on an area formed upon rising ground, and commanding most striking prospects over the principal parts of the domain. These radiating avenues were evidently formed in attention to the fashion set by the French, in that memorable age of continental magnificence, the reign of Louis XIV.

In the deepest recess of the woods is placed a building, designed in imitation of a ruinous pile, and termed ALFRED'S HALL. In the interior is an inscription in Saxon, with a translation into Latin, playing on the fanciful notion that this was the spot upon which King Alfred signed the treaty with Godrun, the Dane, after the defeat of that chief, at *Ethandun*, probably Eddington, in Wiltshire, A.D. 878. It may be almost superfluous to observe that there is no historical authority for such a woodland tale. It has been said that the story on which the conjecture is founded, originated in the similarity of sound between *Achelie*, the antient name of this place, and *Ecglea*, the resting-place of Alfred's army on the night previous to the battle of Ethandun.

It would appear that Pope suggested to Lord Bathurst the plan of this artificial ruin, as the following passage occurs in a letter from Bishop Atterbury to the poet. "May my lord have as much satisfaction in building the house in the wood, and in using it when built, as you have in designing it!" In the time of Pope, the study of architectural antiquities was entirely disregarded by men ambitious of excelling in elegant learning. The hall of Alfred is, consequently, destitute of all approaches to the Saxon style of architecture, and, indeed, like most modern *ruins*, fails to resemble the buildings of any precise æra.

Several minor ornamental erections, in different parts of the grounds, are not entitled to particular notice; but some curiosity will be excited by a real antiquity, in the form of a stone cross, which formerly stood in the market-place of Cirencester. On the capital of the shaft were four shields of arms, now nearly effaced by age. Within the limits of the park is, likewise, a circular tumulus, about twenty feet in height, commonly called *Grismond's Tower*. This tumulus, or barrow, was opened under the direction of the first earl, and was found to contain several large urns, full of ashes and burnt bones.

We must not conclude without observing, that Lord Bathurst had the singular felicity of living to see his vast plantations attain a full degree of vigour and maturity; on which occasion have been applied to him the lines of Claudian, thus translated by Cowley:

A neighbouring wood, born with himself, he sees,
And loves his own contemporary trees.

THE ABBEY HOUSE

9

The Abbey-House, Cirencester

THE SEAT OF MISS MASTER

THIS handsome residence is situated on the northern border of the town of Cirencester, and occupies, with its attached gardens and pleasure-grounds, the site and home demesne of the dissolved abbey of St. Mary.

In presenting a brief historical outline of the monastic foundation at this place, it is necessary to observe that a College of Prebendaries existed here previously to the Norman Conquest, the founders of which institution are now entirely unknown. On the decay of this establishment, an Abbey was founded by King Henry I. for canons regular of the order of St. Augustine. The buildings were commenced in 1117, and completed within the following fourteen years. The endowments, which were considerable, proceeded chiefly from the large possessions of Reinbald, or Rainbaldus, dean of this college, and chancellor to Edward the Confessor; which estates were confirmed to the new foundation by the original charter of Henry I. The abbot sat as a lord of parliament, in the reign of the third Henry; but the heads of this religious house do not appear to have been regularly summoned to the national assembly before the fifteenth century. Amongst the most distinguished abbots must be mentioned Alexander Neccham, who died in 1217, greatly celebrated for the extent of his literary attainments. On the surrender of the Abbey, in 1539, its annual revenues were stated to amount to the large sum of 1051*l*.: 7*s* : 1¼*d*.

We have observed, in a previous page, that the Abbey-buildings were taken down by order of King Henry VIII. By that king the site was bestowed on Roger Bassinge, Esq.; and, in the reservations of the grant, an especial command was inserted that the fabric should be levelled with the ground, and the materials carried away. The exact spot on which the abbey stood is not now to be ascertained, but there are conclusive reasons for believing that it occupied ground to the north of the present parochial church; and it has been thought that the last-named structure was placed within the limits of the monastic cemetery. Concerning the character of the buildings thus destroyed by direction of the barbaric Henry, we know little, except through the intelligence conveyed by Leland, who, in the record of his visit, immediately prior to the demolition of this structure, observes that the eastern division of the Abbey-church was evidently of great antiquity, whilst the parts to the west of the transept were "but new work to speke of." He adds that, in the body of the church, was "a sepulchre Cross, of white marble," with an inscription to the memory of Reinbald, dean of the dissolved collegiate institution. From the same writer it appears that "the hart of Sentia, wife to Richard, King of the Romains, and Erle of Cornwalle" was deposited in this church.

The site of the Abbey, and the contiguous lands granted at the dissolution to Roger Bassinge, having again come into the possession of the crown, were bestowed by King Edward VI. in the first year of his reign, on Thomas, Lord Seymour. On the attainder of that nobleman, they were demised for a term of years, by the same sovereign, to Sir Anthony Kingston, Knight. Queen

Elizabeth, by letters patent, dated on the sixth day of January, in the seventh year of her reign, granted the reversion of these lands to Richard Master, Esq. for the consideration of 590*l*: 16*s*: 3*d*; and the posterity of that gentleman, in a direct line, have enjoyed the estate down to the present day.

This family trace their descent from the family of Master, seated in Kent at an early period. Richard Master, to whom Elizabeth granted the site of Cirencester Abbey, was physician to that queen. Several of the Gloucestershire branch of this respectable family have served the office of high sheriff, and have also represented the county of Gloucester, and the borough of Cirencester, in parliament.

Dr. Richard Master, physician to Queen Elizabeth, erected on the Abbey-lands a substantial and spacious mansion, which constituted the abode of his family until recent years. An engraved view of the antient house, and gardens, is given in the History of Gloucestershire by Sir R. Atkyns; and the whole of the buildings and grounds, as there delineated, curiously exhibit the arrangements, free from innovation, of the ages in which they were erected and laid out. This mansion was honoured with the visits of two regal personages. King Charles I. passed one night here, when on his march from Bristol to Oxford, in August, 1643, and was again entertained by Sir William Master, on his return from Bath, in 1644. It is recorded in the parish register that Queen Anne lay at the Abbey-house, on the night of the 27th of August, 1702.

The proprietors of this seat, through several descents, appear to have acted with commendable attention to the injunctions received by all purchasers of monastic sites, at the time of the dissolution, in respect to the maintenance of hospitality. The local historian, Rudder, informs us that, even in part of the eighteenth century, "here was a kind of open house-keeping at Christmas, for twelve days together." Probably we may, at this place, find one of the last instances in which the rites of hospitality were performed, from a traditional reverence for customs cherished by the antient ecclesiastical lords of the soil.

The good old mansion of the Master family was taken down about the year 1776, partly because it evinced some symptoms of decay, but chiefly on account of its antiquated character; and the present building was shortly after erected, on the same site. The modern house is a substantial square fabric, very genteel and commodious, but deriving its attractions rather from the history of the spot it occupies than from its merits as an architectural object. The large attached grounds (comprising the antient precincts of the Abbey) are laid out with considerable judgment and correctness of taste. In the lawns and umbrageous walks of these pleasure-grounds, as at present disposed, we behold unequivocal improvements effected by those alterations which have swept away, perhaps with too harsh a hand, as regards the buildings, nearly all traces of antient days from a demesne that depends for much of its interest on the tales and recollections of former times.

The large and curious barn, belonging to the home-grange of the Abbey, was taken down a very few years back. Like that at Cholsey, in Berkshire, it was of great antiquity, and much massy timber was used in its construction. A gateway on the borders of the Abbey-grounds is now the only relic of the monastic buildings, worthy of notice. The arch of entrance is semicircular, but entirely destitute of architectural enrichments.

IO

Rendcombe

THE SEAT OF SIR BERKELEY WILLIAM GUISE, BART. M.P.

THE manor of Rendcombe, which had belonged, before the entry of the Normans, to the Saxon Aluric, was given by William I. to Turold, whose son, Gislebert, forfeiting it in rebellion against William Rufus, it was, by that king, bestowed on Robert Fitz-Hamon, Earl of Gloucester. Mabell, the daughter of this nobleman, carried the estate in marriage to Robert, natural son of King Henry I. who was created Earl of Gloucester. William, the son of Earl Robert, had, for his heir, the Lady Amice, his daughter, who was wife of Richard de Clare, ancestor of Gilbert de Clare, who fell at the battle of Bannocksbourne, in the reign of Edward II. Gilbert left no issue, and his estates were divided between his sisters. Rendcombe then became the property of the Lady Margaret, at that time wife of Piers Gaveston, and afterwards of Hugh de Audley. By the second husband she left a daughter, Margaret, wife of Ralph, Lord Stafford. On the attainder of Humphry, Earl of Stafford and Duke of Buckingham, who was slain, in the cause of the house of Lancaster, at the battle of Northampton, Rendcombe was granted by Edward IV. to Richard Nevil, the celebrated Earl of Warwick.

When that earl also fell in civil contest, a grant of this manor was obtained from the crown by the wealthy and distinguished merchant, John Tame, whose name again occurs in our notice of the church and manor of Fairford. He was succeeded by his son, Sir Edmond Tame, whose son Edmond dying without issue, his estates devolved on his three sisters, the eldest of whom was married to Sir Humphry Stafford, and acceded to this manor.

Before the year 1608, the estate was sold by the Staffords to Sir Richard Berkeley. It was again sold by Sir Maurice Berkeley to the father of Sir William Guise; and, under the will of the last baronet of that name, it devolved on the present Sir Berkeley William Guise, Bart. M. P. for the county of Gloucester, and eldest son of Sir John Guise, descended from another branch of this antient family, seated at Highnam, near Gloucester.

The mansion of Rendcombe is distant from the town of Cirencester about six miles, towards the north-west, and is seated on the slope of a gently-swelling eminence, at the base of which flows the river Churn, here a small and tardy stream. The park is of considerable extent, and is enriched by some noble and ornamental spreads of wood.

The topographer has, in regard to this seat, an opportunity, unusually desirable, of viewing representations of the domain, made at several periods in which its features were greatly dissimilar.—In the History of this county by Sir R. Atkyns is an engraved view of Rendcombe, as it appeared early in the eighteenth century. That engraving curiously exhibits the disposal of the grounds in terraces, plots, ponds of formal shape, woods cut into fantastical patterns, vistas of trees, and fountains designed as ornaments. A more modern plate is given in the work by Rudder; and, in the view now presented, it will be seen that the formal labours of those who indulged a perverse taste, by torturing nature into artificial resemblances, are entirely swept away

RENDCOMBE

by the better genius of recent ages. The whole domain is now lovely in natural charms; and a cursory glance must be sufficient to convince the examiner, familiar with the view above noticed, that the dignity, as well as the beauty, of a family-residence, is advanced by such alterations as have been here effected.

The mansion is a square fabric, of a solid and respectable character, well suited to the representative of a family of antient county-standing, and high consideration. In several of the apartments are well-selected paintings, by eminent masters, amongst which are conspicuous some good pictures by Velasquez, Murillo, and Spagnoletto.

The Parochial Church of Rendcombe is in the vicinity of the mansion. This structure was erected under the auspices of the Tame family, and probably by Sir Edmond Tame, who is well known to have completed the fine edifice commenced by his father at Fairford, in this county. In the window of the south chancel are the initials E. T. At the west end rises an embattled tower, partially seen in the annexed view, embowered by the thick woods which form distinguished features in the scenery of Rendcombe.

KING'S WESTON

II

King's Weston

THE SEAT OF THE RIGHT HON. EDWARD SOUTHWELL CLIFFORD, LORD DE CLIFFORD

IN our account of Redland Court we found occasion to mention the luxuriant beauty of the scenery in the environs of Bristol, upon its western side. A considerable part of this district is engrossed by the parish of Henbury, which fine tract abounds in diversities of surface, is richly clothed with ornamental woods, and is watered by the meanders of the river Avon on its south and south-western limits, while the Severn forms its majestic boundary towards the west and north-west. Of this parish King's Weston is a tything.

The principal manor of King's Weston was given by Henry II. to Robert Fitzharding, ancestor of the Berkeley family. Maurice Berkeley, grandson of Robert Fitzharding, assumed the name of Gaunt, but died without male issue, in the fourteenth year of Henry III. and left, as his heiress, an only sister, named Eve, who was married to Anselm de Gurnay. After remaining in this family through several descents, the estate of King's Weston was carried in marriage, by Elizabeth de Gurney, to John ap Adam, in the reign of Edward I. Sir Thomas ap Adam, in the fourth of King Edward III. sold this manor to Sir Maurice Berkeley, who greatly distinguished himself at the memorable siege of Calais. It continued in the Berkeley family until the twelfth of Elizabeth, at which time it was sold, by Sir Richard Berkeley, to Sir William Wintour. In 1614, Sir Edward Wintour sold it to Humphry Hook, an alderman of Bristol, whose son, Sir Humphry Hook, again sold it to Sir Robert Southwell, ancestor of Lord de Clifford.

A minute detail, respecting the annals of the noble family by which this seat is at present possessed, will scarcely be expected in a work professedly treating on topography; but we cannot refrain from reminding the reader that Sir Robert Southwell, who purchased this estate of Sir Humphry Hook, was eminent for talent in public business, and for an exemplary liberality of pursuit in his hours of private enjoyment. He had been confidentially employed in affairs of state by Charles II. but declined an active interference in politics during the greater part of the succeeding reign, and passed those years of wise retirement in philosophical studies at this mansion. His successful cultivation of science, and habits of association with persons engaged in similar pursuits, caused him to be several times chosen president of the Royal Society.—On the rise of a brighter day in the political hemisphere, his powers were speedily called into action, and he was constituted, by King William, principal Secretary of State for Ireland. That sovereign honoured King's Weston with his presence, on the 6th September, 1690. On that day his majesty landed from Ireland, in which country he had recently achieved his important victory on the banks of the Boyne. He had been attended thither, as an adherent equally faithful in the hour of danger and triumph, by Sir Robert Southwell; and the doors of this mansion were never opened on a more memorable occasion, than that of receiving the royal master of their owner, on his return from so signal an engagement as that which decided the fate of three kingdoms. King William slept here, on the night of September 6th. On the following day he departed for Badminton, the seat of the Duke of Beaufort.

Edward Southwell, son of Sir Robert, was also highly distinguished in public business; and his name, as chief secretary to the Lord Lieutenant of Ireland, stands connected with many weighty transactions of state in that country.

The present Baron de Clifford is grandson of secretary Southwell. The father of his lordship was admitted to the baronies of de Clifford, Westmorland, and Vesci, upon the decease of his aunt, Margaret, Countess of Leicester, and Baroness de Clifford, in 1775.

The antient mansion of King's Weston is said, by some writers, to have been erected by Inigo Jones. An engraving of that seat is given by Sir R. Atkyns, from which it appears to have been an irregular pile, having, for its principal features, many angular pediments, and two lofty turrets, crowned with vanes. Along the principal front was a line of embattled parapet. The trees throughout the grounds, were chiefly disposed in straight rows; and the gardens, which Atkyns terms "delightful," were laid out in topiary with boundary-hedges cut to imitate massive walls, and shrubs shaped to the resemblance of pyramids.

The old house was, either wholly or in its principal parts, taken down early in the last century, and a new structure erected, after the designs of Sir John Vanbrugh. Important alterations, however, have been made, under the direction of the late Mr. Mylne; and, in a biographical account of that architect, we find the following passage. "Being employed by Mr. Southwell to alter his splendid mansion at King's Weston, Mr. Mylne commenced his operations by a plan of the house. Whilst thus occupied he discovered a small room, to which there were no means of access; and, on cutting into it, they found a quantity of old plate, together with *the records of a barony*, granted to the family by Henry III. The apartment had, probably, been shut up during the rebellion against Charles I."

The house of King's Weston is situated on elevated ground, and encompassed by a park, of noble extent and exquisite beauty. This is usually styled one of Vanbrugh's best works, and it certainly has the merit of greater simplicity than is observable in most of his palatial and domestic buildings. We here find few of those efforts at extrinsic ornament, so wantonly employed, at Blenheim and some other places, by this architect. The attractions of the pile proceed solely from the amplitude and harmony of its proportions and respective parts. The character of the building is weighty, but the effect is commanding. The residence seems formed for the use of nobility; but, with most spectators, the exterior will rather be approved than admired. With so fine a site, and the ample resources of the Southwell family at his command, the architect of Castle-Howard should, certainly, have produced a structure of a more decisive character, and better assimilated to the lovely scenery by which his work is surrounded. As a minor subject of commendation, it has been remarked, by the editors of the Beauties of England, that "a peculiarity, and perhaps a merit, in Vanbrugh's architecture, was his management of chimneys, the purpose of which he concealed by uniting them with the mass, so as to improve the general effect." At this place the chimneys are connected in an arcade, placed centrally in the roofing.

The interior is divided into very numerous apartments, many of which reflect much credit on the judgment and taste of the architect, under whose care the building was, in a great measure, reformed. Few, however, are of large dimensions, with the exception of the hall, which is a fine and lofty room, well finished, and appropriately adorned with an extensive collection of family-portraits. From an inner-hall proceeds the grand staircase, which is extremely elegant, and much ornamented with good carving.

The numerous portraits of the De Clifford and Southwell families, involve the representations of several persons interesting from their connexion with the history of the country at large; and the principal rooms are enriched with many excellent paintings, by some of the most esteemed old masters, on subjects of general attraction. Among these are works by Guido, Guercino, Maratti, Domenichino, Rubens, and Poussin. The portraits comprise several by Holbein, including a fine picture of *Sir Richard Southwell*, a statesman of eminence in the reign of the eighth Henry, and one of the overseers of that sovereign's last will. Inserted in the doors of two cabinets is a valuable collection of miniature portraits, representing many distinguished persons, from the time of Queen Elizabeth to that of James II.

The park is nearly five hundred acres in extent, and possesses a happy combination of most of the principal requisites in picturesque beauty. The surface is finely varied, and the wood abundant and of luxuriant growth. At the extremity of a vale, two miles in width, and prolific of charms throughout every rood, is viewed the river Severn, here a mimic-sea, enlivened by shipping, and receiving into its broad bosom the tributary waters of the Avon. On the opposite coast, the mountains of Wales rise, in gradations and varieties hesitating between the sublime and the lovely. The frequent knolls in this delightful park are not only in themselves estimable objects, but give facilities of varied prospect to the lover of the picturesque; and the lawns, which invite the progress of the examiner, would seem to be spread with unusual softness.

In a poem termed Clifton, written by Mr. Jones, are the following, among other verses, intended to convey ideas of the charms here presented. If not worthy of the subject, the lines of the votive poet of this fair district should still be held in remembrance, whilst we discuss its claims on admiration:

> The vale incult, by random robe see grac'd,
> With SOUTHWELL soaring to the mark of taste;
> Whose classic eye each erring stroke shall scan,
> Reform the model, and improve the plan;
> To simple majesty reduce the pile,
> And bid discretion through the garden smile;
> Make truth and unity in all combine,
> And taste end judgment crown the clear design;
> Unnumber'd beauties thence attract the soul,
> That seem expanded to the distant pole;
> The outline endless, charms th' insatiate eyes,
> Within that trait ten thousand beauties rise,
> With incidents above SALVATOR's hand,
> Of ocean, air, of forest, sky, and land.

BARNSLEY PARK

12

Barnsley Park

THE SEAT OF SIR JAMES MUSGRAVE, BART.

THE village of Barnsley is distant four miles from Cirencester, on the road leading to Oxford. The mansion of Sir James Musgrave is situated in the southern part of an extensive park, on the north side of this rural, although road-side, village.

Barnsley is mentioned in the Book of Domesday, as a manor dependant on Beckberie (Bibury) and was at that time held by Durand, of Ulstan, bishop of Worcester. Shortly after the Conquest, the property, then divided into two manors, was possessed by the families of De Bohun and Herbert, with whom it remained until the reign of Edward I. at which time the manors were united, and the property was acquired, by Hugh le Despencer. On the attainder of Despencer it lapsed to the crown, whence it was re-granted, in the first year of Edward III. to Edmond, Earl of Kent, at which date it was stated to be of the annual value of £22. In its descent through the successors of this earl, it came, by default of male issue in John Earl of Kent, to Joan his sister, well known in history, under the name of the *Fair Maid of Kent*, who was then wife of Sir Thomas Holland, and was afterwards married to Edward the Black Prince. That lady died in the ninth year of the reign of her son, Richard II.; and the manor of Barnsley then passed to Thomas Holland, Earl of Kent, her son by her first husband. Eleanor, coheiress to the family of Holland, carried it, in marriage, to Roger Mortimer, Earl of March, with whose family it subsequently merged in the crown, whence it was alienated to the Tames, of Fairford. From that successful trading family it passed to Thomas Morton, whose grandson, William, had, for his coheiress, Dorothy his sister. That lady married Ralph Johnson, by whom the estate was sold to William Bourchier.

The Bourchier family resided on this manor through several generations, and are said to have at one time occupied an antient building, situated near the middle of the village. Brereton Bourchier, Esq. was the last proprietor of this name, and resided, as we are told by Sir R. Atkyns, in "a large new house, having a pleasant grove, a large park, and walks of trees." Catharine, his widow, remarried with Henry Perrott, Esq. whose daughter and surviving coheir, Cassandra, devised the estate to her nearest relative, James Musgrave, Esq. father of Sir James Musgrave, Bart. the present possessor of this domain.

The "new house," mentioned by Sir R. Atkyns, was not calculated for long duration. The history of Gloucestershire, by Atkyns, was published in 1712, and the house of the Bourchiers, although recently erected, gave place, about the year 1730, to a fresh structure, raised under the auspices of Henry Perrott, Esq. then lord of the manor of Barnsley. This is a spacious and elegant building, aptly described, in the Beauties of England, as "a sumptuous edifice, in the high Italian style."

It will be much doubted whether the Italian mode of design, which Lord Burlington so fondly laboured to render familiar in this country, is adapted either to our climate or manners. Still less does it, in general, assimilate with the scenery of England. Buildings in this style are, therefore, usually viewed as gorgeous curiosities, made to be looked at rather than to be enjoyed; or as natural exotics, which we admire in the conservatory, but with the alloy of a conviction that they are to be seen to full advantage in their native country alone. The antient English style, on the other hand, accords with our oaken woods, expansive downs, and beech-covered hills, without doors; whilst, on the interior, the large and grand, but warm and sheltering rooms, seem genial to the vicissitudes of an island-climate.

The fine building now under notice is one of the most pleasing examples, that we have seen, of a style of building, which is, assuredly, captivating, if exercised under the favour of serene skies and an unclouded sun. Several apartments display considerable taste, and are at once rich, light, and beautiful. The surrounding park contains not less than three hundred and fifty acres, and is abundantly wooded.

Within the parish of Barnsley are large quarries of freestone, of an excellent quality.

The Parochial Church is said to have been erected by Sir Edmond Tame early in the sixteenth century; and it may he remarked that, according to a current tradition, the antient inn of the village was built for the accommodation of that knight, whilst he was engaged in superintending the erection of this church and the church of Rendcombe. The benefice is a rectory, in the peculiar of Bibury, but the patronage is annexed to the manor.

13

Frampton Court

THE SEAT OF HENRY CLIFFORD-CLIFFORD, ESQ.

FRAMPTON, often termed Frampton-upon-Severn, a village of peculiar attractions, is situated upon the eastern borders of the river Severn, at the distance of ten miles from the City of Gloucester. This estate is the antient property of the family of Clifford, so named from the castle of Clifford, in Herefordshire; which family deduces its origin from the sovereign Dukes of Normandy. William, son of Richard, Duke of Normandy, had issue, among other sons, Richard, who entered England with the army of the conqueror, and was father of Walter, first Lord Clifford. This family possessed the manor of "Frantone" when the record of Domesday was formed. Walter, the above-named Lord Clifford, had two sons and two daughters, the younger of whom has attained much historical and romantic celebrity, as the "Fair Rosamond" of King Henry II. Lord Clifford bestowed this estate on Richard, his second son, whose descendants settled at this place. The manor in successive ages, passed, by females, to the Fitz-Paynes, Chidiocks, and Arundels. In the year 1634, it was sold by Sir John Arundel to Sir Thomas Hooke; from the representative of whose daughter and co-heir, Elizabeth, wife of Thomas Grove, it was purchased by the late Nathaniel Clifford, Esq. and annexed to a considerable estate, which he inherited from a branch of the Cliffords, and which had never been alienated since the time of their ancestor, the possessor at the date of Domesday.

The descent of the mansion and attached grounds, distinct from the manor, may be briefly traced in the following terms, as regards recent ages.—John Clifford, the last male heir of that branch of his ancient family which had resided at Frampton through many generations, died in 1671, leaving two daughters, the eldest of whom succeeded him at this place, and married Nathaniel Clutterbuck, Esq. Richard Clutterbuck, grandson of the gentleman last named, died unmarried; and his sister and heir married William Bell, of Gloucester, and of Sainthurst, in this county, Esq. The daughter and heir of Mr. Bell married Nathaniel Winchcombe, Esq. and left an only son and heir, who, in 1801, was authorized, by royal sign manual, to use the name and bear the arms of Clifford. He was succeeded by his only son, Henry Clifford-Clifford Esq. the present proprietor of this estate.

The antient manor-house of the Clifford family occupied the site of the present mansion. That building was not engraved for the work by Sir Robert Atkyns, and we believe that little is now known concerning its architectural character. That it was both a capacious and a strong fabric is evinced by the circumstance of its having received a garrison, on the side of the parliamentarians, in the civil war of the seventeenth century.

The antient house was taken down about the year 1731, at which time the present mansion was erected, by order of Richard Clutterbuck, Esq. The building is equally creditable to the talents of the architect, and the judgment of his employer. It consists of a centre and lateral pavilions, the whole being of just and pleasing proportions. The house shows two fronts. The

FRAMPTON COURT

principal doorway is approached by a wide and lofty flight of steps, and the chief front of the central structure is plentifully ornamented, but not with any obvious redundance of decoration. In the frontispiece four pilasters sustain an angular pediment. No deviation occurs from the simple grandeur of Grecian architecture, and the entire building, as regards the era in which it was designed, is suited, in every particular, to the residence of that most estimable character, the country gentleman of England. We regret that the name of the architect is not known, but the design partakes considerably of Vanbrugh's best style. The principal apartments are spacious, and are finished with much elegance. The paintings are not numerous, but it is with peculiar gratification that we find, on a spot so long occupied by the Clifford family, a curious and truly valuable portrait of the fair and unfortunate Rosamond. The artist is unknown, but the picture, independent of its locality, is of great interest.—In regard to the subject of this painting, the present writer will take the freedom of observing, that, in the "Beauties of Oxfordshire," he has entered, at some length, into an examination of the historical anecdotes connected with this Rose of the Cliffords, who sank the victim of unusual circumstances, and retired to religious seclusion when the marriage of King Henry destroyed her last hope of regaining tranquillity, by the reparation of her honour.

Frampton Court is surrounded by a park and pleasure-grounds, about seventy acres in extent. In noticing the adjuncts of this very respectable seat, it is necessary that we should convey some idea respecting the character of the dependant village, the principal features of which are most agreeably blended with the arrangement and display of the manorial demesne. This elegant, although strictly rural, village, is built round a green, of an oblong or oval form. Nearly the whole of one long side is occupied by the seat and its appendages, whilst the opposite side is lined with houses and cottages, generally of a pleasing aspect, and often detached, with surrounding plots of garden-ground. At one end of the oval stands the church, which was chiefly built in the year 1315, and contains the ashes of many of the Cliffords. At the other end of the green is the parsonage-house.

This combination of objects—the sacred, the grand, and the simple—in one harmonious grouping of village scenery, is an unusual, and a very beautiful, feature of English topography. The picture thus formed is more imperative over the fancy, and likewise over some of the best feelings of the spectator, even than it is pleasing to the eye. It is a panorama for the heart; and delights us, beyond the reach of all charms merely pictorial, with ideas of the resident country gentleman, surrounded by his tenants and friends, and courting the reciprocal advantages of an association with rural neighbourhood.

WILLIAMSTRIP

14

Williamstrip

THE SEAT OF MICHAEL HICKS BEACH, ESQ.

WILLIAMSTRIP is a hamlet to the parish of Coln St. Alwyn's. The antient name of this hamlet was Willasthorpe; which appellation was first corrupted to Williamstrop, and afterwards to Williamstrip. The property, which had previously been divided between the Abbey of Bruerne and Sir Walter Dennis, passed, as parcel of Bruerne Abbey, to Sir Edmond Tame, whose sister and coheir, Alice, carried it to her husband, Thomas Verney; from whom it descended to their grandson George. It is presumed to have then passed by purchase to William Powle, Esq. Catherine, the only daughter and heir of Henry Powle, Esq. speaker of the house of commons, and master of the rolls, in the reign of William III., married Henry Ireton, Esq., who resided at Williamstrip in the year 1712. Having no issue, she devised the contiguous manors of Quennington and Williamstrip to John, son of her uncle, Sir Richard Powle, with remainder, in default of issue, to her cousin, William Forrester, Esq., who accordingly succeeded, on the decease of John Powle. By Mr. Forrester the estate was sold to Humphry Mackworth Praed, Esq. who again sold it to Samuel Blackwell, Esq.; which gentleman resided here in 1770. It was subsequently purchased by Michael Hicks Beach, Esq. the present proprietor.

Among the plates by Kip, inserted in the history of this county by Sir Robert Atkyns, is a view of the house of Williamstrip, as it appeared when it formed the seat of Mr. Ireton. The fabric, as there represented, exhibits several architectural peculiarities. The roofs, which were in the Dutch style of building, were extremely curious. The slope from the parapet terminated in a flat area; at each corner of which was a chimney. The offices were very extensive, and had an unusual number of large and long windows. The whole upper story of these offices was occupied by sleeping rooms, for domestics. In the roof was the same kind of flat area as that of the main building, along which stood a row of chimneys. At one gable was a door of extraordinary dimensions, with a very large garret-projection of the roof above. By the side of the iron gates at the carriage entrance, was a lodge, of a dull and heavy character, roofed like the other buildings, but with Tuscan pilasters at the angles, and having no door towards the gate.

The existing mansion was built early in the eighteenth century, but has been enlarged and altered at several times. It is a capacious and firmly-built pile, but quite destitute of pretensions to architectural elegance, and must be described as a large, roomy, and convenient family-house, rather than as an ornamental structure. Though not calculated externally to gratify the eye of taste, and deficient in many of the architectural characteristics, both of the dignified mansion and the rural villa, this is a house of commanding magnitude, and the interior is well suited to the accommodation of a large establishment. The pictures are chiefly family portraits. The building is agreeably situated, and the attached grounds are adorned with timber and plantations, judiciously disposed.

The parish of Coln St. Alwyn, to which Williamstrip is a hamlet, is in the vicinity of the town of Fairford, at the distance of twenty-three miles from the city of Gloucester. This place is situated on the Roman road, termed the Akeman Street (not the Iknield Street, as is asserted in the histories of Gloucestershire); remains of which road, lying in a high ridge, are visible in several parts of the parish. One of the antient British *salt-ways* also passed through this place. The Akeman Street enters the parish from Oxfordshire, and afterwards proceeds to Cirencester, Rodmarton, and Cherrington. The Saltway comes from Droitwich, and appears to have passed the Avon near Evesham. It then bore towards the chain of hills above Sudeley Castle, and thence proceeds by Northleach to this parish, in its way to the sea-coast of Hampshire.

15

Bowden Hall

THE SEAT OF JAMES H. BYLES, ESQ.

THE very desirable residence of Mr. Byles is situated in the parish of Upton St. Leonard, at the distance of rather less than four miles from the city of Gloucester.

This parish (formerly denominated *Optune*) was a member of the extensive manor of Bertune, or Barton, at the time of the Domesday Survey, and is entered in that record among the estates of the crown. The historians of Gloucestershire trace the descent of two antient manors in this parish, both of which were recognised by the name of Upton. Walkelyn de Fabrica "held Uptone of King Edward I. by the service of paying 200 arrow heads." Another manor under this name belonged, for many ages, to the Berkeley family. The manorial privileges are now possessed by the freeholders, but there are also two reputed manors within the parochial limits, respectively termed *Bullins*, and *Grove Court*. The latter was formerly the property of a family which appears to have derived its surname from this estate. "Geoffrey *De Grave* held one yard land in Upton, in the fifth of Henry III. by the service of attending the king in his wars against Wales, with bow and arrows, forty days at his own expense, and afterwards at the cost of the king."

The vale of Gloucester, which extends about fifteen miles from north to south, and from seven to eight miles in a contrary direction, here exhibits some of its most beautiful features. The surface of the country is finely unequal, and is rich in verdure and in varied cultivation; whilst the Severn, increasing in width as it pursues a south-western course, and speedily becoming a river of noble expansion, exhilirates, diversifies, and imparts countless picturesque charms to the scenery.

Bowden Hall is seated on the northern acclivity of one of the hills which rise, with lovely grandeur, from this vale, in the vicinity of Gloucester. The house is a handsome building, erected about fifty years ago, by Robert Campbell, Esq. on an estate purchased by that gentleman of the late Sir John Guise, Bart. The proportions are good, the dimensions capacious, and the whole design is well adapted to an English inland villa, of the most respectable class. The pleasure-grounds are laid out with much good taste, and the house is surrounded by about one hundred acres of richly-wooded land, the property of Mr. Byles, who purchased this estate a few years back. Exquisite views are obtained, in many directions, from the windows of the house, and from various points of the contiguous grounds.

Bowden Hall

16

Matson House

THE SEAT OF MRS. NIBLETT

THIS interesting residence is situated at the foot of Robins'-wood hill, and is distant about two miles from the city of Gloucester. We have, in a previous page, slightly, adverted to the hill which shelters the mansion and village of Matson; but some materials towards a more full description than is there given, may be desirable whilst discussing the present article.

Robins'-wood (in popular phraseology *Robin Hood's*) hill, forms a distinguished feature in the scenery contiguous to the city of Gloucester. Its name is derived from the family of Robins, who were, for many ages, lessees of the manor of Matson, first under the abbey, and afterwards the chapter, of Gloucester. This hill rises from the vale in a conical form, and affords a beautiful object throughout a vast expanse of surrounding country. It is verdant to the summit; and spiral walks, of great extent, are cut on its sides. The prospects obtained from different points, are eminently fine and various. Some writers assert that, in ages previous to the Norman Conquest, it yielded large quantities of iron ore for the use of the forges at Gloucester. Mr. Rudge observes that not any scoria, or cinders, have been here found, the existence of which is usually considered as the proof of antient blomaries having been worked; but several of the springs which issue from its sides, would appear to show that iron ore still forms a large part of the contents of this elevation.

Its springs, however, are not uniformly of this description. The hill of Robins'-wood has, for upwards of four centuries, supplied Gloucester with water, of a pure and excellent quality, which is conveyed to that city by means of pipes. The antiquity of this supply is proved by the following circumstance, which stands on satisfactory record.—William Gerard, styled de Matesden, having granted, in the reign of Edward II., the privilege of conveying water from this hill to the friary of Gloucester, a dispute arose between that religious house and the abbey, as to the quantity the former was to receive: which disagreement was arranged by Edward the Black Prince, in the year 1357.

This place is not mentioned in Domesday; but we are told, by Atkyns, that the manor was held of Humphry de Bohun, Earl of Hereford, and of Joan his wife, in the forty-sixth of Edward III. William Nottingham, attorney-general under Edward IV., gave it, in the tenth year of that king, to the abbey of Gloucester. At the dissolution it was granted to the chapter.

The estate which forms the subject of the present article, was unconnected with abbatial property, and was possessed by the priory of Lanthony. Under the name of "Mattisdon Manor-house," this estate was granted by the crown, in the thirty-fourth Henry VIII., to the corporation of Gloucester; who alienated it, in the following year, to Thomas Lane, Esq. From him it speedily passed to Richard Pate; and again from this proprietor to Richard Ligon, who had livery of it in the ninth of Queen Elizabeth; shortly after which date it was conveyed to the family of Selwyn. In consequence, of a marriage between Jasper Selwyn, and Margaret, daughter and

Matson House

coheir of Thomas Robins, lessee of the manor, both estates became united in this family, and descended to the late witty and eccentric George Augustus Selwyn, Esq. who represented the city of Gloucester in many successive parliaments. On the decease of that gentleman, in 1791, this property devolved to Thomas Townshend, Viscount Sydney, maternally descended from the Selwyns, by the marriage of Charles, second Viscount Townshend, with Albinia, daughter of Colonel John Selwyn, of this place.

The mansion is a building of some antiquity, and is usually said to have been erected in the reign of Elizabeth, by Sir Ambrose Willoughby. We regret to state that it has been modernized, with too little attention to its original architectural character. In this respect the house of Matson shares the fate of many venerable structures, in various parts of England; and the neglect of *keeping,* in alterations of such buildings, cannot be too strongly reprehended, as an equal increase of light, and elegance of accommodation, might be obtained without the least sacrifice of architectural propriety. It is to be hoped that the reign of innovation, in this particular, is now drawing towards a close, and will soon entirely disappear, before that taste for the ornamental character of antient domestic architecture, which was rendered in some degree fashionable by the writings and buildings of Horace Walpole, and has been successfully cultivated by the late James Wyatt, and the present very judicious architect Mr. Wyatville.

In this house King Charles I. quartered during the siege of Gloucester, in 1643. His majesty took possession of these quarters on the night of the 10th of August; having, on the morning of that day (to use the words of John Corbet) "come in person before the town, that the terror of his presence might prevail with some, and the person of the king amaze the simple, and seem to alter the case." Unprepared to encounter Essex, who was hastening to the relief of the city, the king retired from Matson on the 5th of September following; and the gloom of a rainy and tempestuous night was added to the comfortless circumstances under which he quitted this temporary abode.

The grounds attached to the mansion are of a pleasing, but secluded character. The chief windows open to a lawn and grove; and the whole of the demesne presents a fine picturesque shade.

CERNEY HOUSE

17

Cerney House

THE SEAT OF WILLIAM CROOME, ESQ.

THE parish of North Cerney is situated in the Cotswold district, at the distance of four miles from Cirencester. The river Churn passes through this parish, and imparts much fertility to the meadows along which it flows.

THE manorial history of Cerney is subject to some confusion, the manors having been divided, at an early period, between the abbey of Abingdon; the tenants of that religious foundation; the earls of Gloucester; and the archbishops of York. Two distinct estates are mentioned in Domesday; one of which was held, as in the reign of Edward the Confessor, by St. Oswald's Priory, Gloucester; and the other, in that reign, by Elaf and his brother, but at the time of the survey by Gislebert, the son of Turold. The last named proprietor was once of considerable influence in this part of Gloucestershire; and, in addition to this estate, possessed the adjoining fine property of Rendcombe. He took side with Robert Curtoise in opposing King William II.; and, on the unsuccessful termination of their efforts, his English estates were seized by the crown, and subsequently became vested in the family of de Clare.

The manor which had appertained to the archbishops of York was granted, in the sixth of Edward VI. to Sir Thomas Chamberlaine; but it appears to have been quickly alienated, as in 1608, it was possessed by the family of Partridge. In 1712, it was divided between persons named Combs and Oatridge, of whom it was purchased by Earl Bathurst.

The estate on which Cerney House is erected, belonged, for several ages, to the family of Rich. Of this property William Rich died seized, in the fifteenth of Charles I.; and it is stated by Sir R. Atkyns that Mr. Rich had a good house here, in 1712. Edward Pickering Rich, Esq. left an infant son and heir, for whose benefit this estate was sold, in the year 1760; at which time it was purchased by Thomas Tyndale, Esq. The present mansion was built in 1780, by Colonel Tyndale, son of that gentleman, and was successively in the possession of William Kimber, Barrington Price, and John Hooper Holder, Esquires. By Mr. Holder the mansion and a contiguous estate were sold, in 1814, to the present proprietor, William Croome, Esq. This very handsome seat is surrounded by a park and pleasure-grounds, comprising nearly one hundred acres.—The manorial rights of the tithing of Woodmancotte, in which this estate is situated, are vested in Sir Berkeley W. Guise, Bart.

The Church of North Cerney contains some remains of painted glass, and a stone pulpit, finely carved. Sir Robert Atkyns mentions "the statue of a priest, in his robes, in a niche in the south wall of the chancel;" but this monumental statue has been some time removed. In the church-yard are the base and shaft of a cross.

Near the western extremity of Cerney Farm are the traces of an encampment, appearing to be Roman, which are noticed by Mr. Bigland as "the imperfect vestiges of a Roman Specula, or out-post, with circumvallations." About one century back, a lachrymatory, of a blue vitrified substance, was dug from the soil in Calmsden-field.

C<small>OTSWOLD</small> H<small>OUSE</small>

18

Cotswold House

THIS seat, like that which forms the subject of the preceding article, is situated in the parish of North Cerney, and was purchased of William Veel, Esq. by the late Robert Milligan, Esq. in the year 1808. The residence is a modern stone building, finely placed on the slope of one of the Cotswold Hills, and the attached grounds are richly and judiciously planted. The front of the house looks down on one of those lovely valleys which are so often found in this unequal, and fertile district, and commands extensive views over the country beyond it.

The late proprietor, Robert Milligan, Esq. (who died in 1809, leaving this estate to his daughters), was a West India merchant of high eminence, and a man distinguished for energy of mind and liberality of sentiment. To him the city of London is principally indebted for that great public work, the West India Docks, by which the interests of that branch of commerce, and the security of the revenue, have been so materially promoted.

The first stone was laid in the year 1800, and so unremitting were the exertions used in conducting the undertaking, that the Docks were opened for the admission of ships in the course of two years after their commencement. In proof of the high sense entertained of his services by the directors and proprietors of this establishment, a bronze statue, executed by Westmacott, was erected to his memory, at their expense, and placed at the entrance to the Docks. The following inscription is engraved upon the pedestal:

To perpetuate on this spot
The Memory of
ROBERT MILLIGAN,
A Merchant of London,
To whose Genius, Perseverance, and Guardian Care
The surrounding great Work principally owes
Its Design, Accomplishment, and Regulations;
The Directors and Proprietors,
Deprived by his Death,
On the 21st of May, 1809,
Of the continuance of his valuable services,
By their unanimous Vote
Have caused this Statue to be erected.

In the topographical account of Middlesex, forming part of the Beauties of England and Wales, the present writer has found an appropriate page for more extended remarks on the merits of this distinguished BRITISH MERCHANT, and the great work which owes its origin to his genius, and its successful completion to his soundness of judgment and activity of public spirit.

COLESBORNE

19

Colesbourne House

THE SEAT OF HENRY ELWES, ESQ.

THE parish of Colesbourne is situated on the river Churn. The village is placed in a retired valley, to the east of the road leading from Cheltenham to Cirencester, at the distance of six miles from the former town. An eminence in this parish, termed *Colesbourne-pen*, is usually said to be the highest ground in the county

At the time of the Norman Survey the manor of Colesbourne was possessed by the church of Worcester; but was held of that church by Walter, "the brother of Roger."—Milo, the son of Walter, gave the greater part of this estate to the Priory of Lanthony; which religious brotherhood obtained a charter of free warren in the twenty-first of Edward I. By Queen Elizabeth the manor was granted, in the sixth year of her reign, to Thomas Reeve and others; and was soon afterwards alienated to William Riggs, in whose family it continued until 1680, at which time it was sold to Philip Sheppard, Esq. John, the descendant of Philip Sheppard, alienated it, in 1770, to Francis Eyre, Esq.; who, about the year 1790, resold to John Elwes, Esq. in whose family the estate is at present vested.

Sir Robert Atkyns describes "Mr. Philip Sheppard, second son of Philip Sheppard, of Hampton, Esq. as having," (about the year 1712) "a good seat near the church;" and observes that there was an antient farm-house, with a chapel adjoining to it, called the Priory. This, we may safely conclude, had constituted a cell to the Priory of Lanthony.

The manor-house, of which we present an engraving, is a modern building, agreeably situated in the hamlet of Rapsgate.

In a division of this parish, termed the *North Field*, are traces of an encampment; and, on a part of the estate of *Combe-end*, were excavated, in 1779 and 1787, the remains of two Roman villas. Some particulars concerning the first of these discoveries have been conveyed in the following words:—"These vestiges contained a pavement, 56 feet long, and 14 broad, with the tessellated pavement of a room close adjoining to it. This was probably a *triclinium*, or entertaining room; especially as near to it was discovered a range of six small apartments, each about twelve feet square, with two larger rooms at one end, and an hypocaust at the other. Among the ruins were found tiles, of a rhomboidal form, in which were the iron nails which fastened them; fragments of glass; and columns."

For a further account of these Roman antiquities we refer to Archæologia, v. ix. p.319, where a plate is given; and to King's Munimenta Antiqua.

BLAISE CASTLE

20

Blaise Castle

THE SEAT OF JOHN S. HARFORD, ESQ. D.C.L. F.R.S.

THE charms of Henbury, proceeding much from rich and tasteful culture, but more from natural beauty, have called forth our warm admiration whilst endeavouring to communicate some ideas respecting the scenery of King's Weston. —In the sedate truth of a reflective hour, and long after the first enthusiasm created by an inspection of this neighbourhood has subsided, we have no hesitation in asserting that the north-western environs of Bristol, and particularly such tracts as lie within the parochial limits of Henbury, are not excelled, in happy combinations of picturesque attributes, by any part of South Britain, however highly praised by poetical tourists or loco-descriptive versifiers. Conspicuous amidst this magnificent display of nature and art, BLAISE HILL lifts its conical form, looking over a world of beauties, and itself constituting a prominent feature in a great variety of landscapes.

This lofty elevation derives its name from a chapel which formerly stood here, and which was dedicated to St. Blasius. It is well known to antiquaries, as having constituted one of the posts of the Dobuni against the Silures, and as having, probably, been re-fortified by Ostorius. On the south side the hill is impregnable, from its steepness; but, in other directions, it has been defended by at least two banks and ditches, which are now over-grown with wood, and are not easily to be traced. An antient stoned road is observable up the north-east side, at the top of which is an entrance; and there is another entrance towards King's Weston Hill. The shape of the fortifications is irregular, and coincides with that of the ground. Some further remarks upon this subject may be seen in the 19th volume of Archæologia, and we may rationally concur with Mr. Fosbroke in believing that the fortifications on this hill were designed to cover the passage at Aust, and to guard it front the invasions of the Silures, on the opposite shore of the Severn. Near the seat of Mr. Harford is, also, a fine camp, having triple ramparts, which imparts the name of *Henbury* to the parish in which it is situated, and which is by some writers supposed to be the Abone of the Romans.

The transcendent attractions of this spot induced Mr. Farr, a tasteful merchant of Bristol, to erect a pleasure-house here, in the year 1766. Some circumstances connected with which undertaking are thus stated, in the "Chronological Outline of the History of Bristol," recently published by Mr. John Evans. "This had been a favourite scene of Mr. Farr's shooting excursions, when a schoolboy; and, to the credit of his decision of character, no less than of his fine taste, in being the first to appreciate the beauties of this spot, it should not be forgotten that he, thus early, determined, whenever he might possess the means and opportunity, to become its purchaser, and make it emulate, as far as its limits would permit, the charms of the far-famed Piercefield estate; with the owner of which, the lamented Valentine Morris, Mr. Farr's family were on terms of intimacy. When the propitious era of maturity and competence arrived, Mr. Farr commenced his operations by laying out a walk around the wood, and opening the foliage at places of easy access, for the most striking points of view. In 1766, at an expense of about 3000*l*., he erected, on the highest acclivity, a castellated building, consisting of a very large circular room and a few small rooms; which he named *Blaise Castle*."—We are enabled to complete this narrative, hut we regret to say that the conclusion is of an unpleasing character. Falling a victim to that mutability of human affairs, to which the mercantile world is especially liable, Mr. Farr, in the year 1778, was no longer able to indulge his taste for elegant retirement, and was constrained to sell this favourite retreat, which was purchased by Denham Skeate, D.C.L. The excellent taste displayed by Mr. Farr, and the peculiar beauties of his place on Blaise Hill, were celebrated in several poetical effusions. The following lines, from the poem of " Clifton," by Mr. Jones, may be cited as a specimen.

> Here FARR, with willing heart, can frequent blend
> The connoisseur, the merchant, and the friend;
> At the rich genial board in each can shine,
> And make his converse lively as his wine.

Dr. Skeate resided here for several years, but without effecting any alterations of importance; and, in 1789, the estate was purchased of that gentleman by the late John S. Harford, Esq. to whom, in conjunction with the present proprietor, the demesne is indebted for the greater part of its embellishments. Mr. Harford added considerably to the extent of the territory; and, about the year 1795, erected the existing spacious and elegant mansion. This beautiful structure cannot be too highly commended, for the excellence of its proportions, and the exquisite simplicity of its design. The material is stone; and, where ornament is used, the order has been judiciously adopted. Mr. Paty was the architect employed, and he received, in his professional exertions, the assistance of Mr. Nash. Great praise is due to their conjoined efforts; and we must, also, hold in remembrance that the taste of the employer is ever, in a great degree, entitled to applause for the furtherance of a correct and appropriate design, or responsible for a large share of the opprobium cast on a building having an opposite character. A writer, therefore, bestows tacit and honest commendation on the taste of the family under whose auspices a mansion is erected, when he pronounces the structure, as in the present instance, to be simple, classical, and truly elegant.

A love of the arts is manifested in every part of the internal arrangement. The present Mr. Harford, during a long residence in Italy, formed a valuable collection of pictures, which now adorn the estimable seat at which he resides. Among these the following are the most conspicuous.

> *Deposition from the Cross*. Michael Angelo Buanorotti. From the Borghese Gallery, Rome
> *Entombment of Christ*. Daniel de Volterra.
> *Holy Family*. Michael Angelo and Sebastian del Piombo. From the Boschi Palace, Rome.
> *Virgin in Adoration* over the infant Saviour. Corregio.
> *St. Veronica*, Guido.
> *Christ and the Woman of Samaria*. Carlo Dolce. From the collection of the late Earl of
>   Suffolk.
> *Holy Family*. Parmagiano. From the Barberini Gallery, Rome.

There are, also, in this collection, several fine landscapes by Gaspar Poussin and Salvator Rosa.

The character of the whole demesne of Blaise Hill is strongly marked by the romantic and picturesque. The approach to the house is conducted through a woody glen, which forms the most striking feature of the place, and bears much resemblance to several admired ravines in Ireland. This tasteful and bold undertaking was partly executed under the direction of the late Mr. Repton; but great improvements on the line laid down by that architect and landscape-gardener, have been recently effected by Mr. Harford, and the road now constitutes one of the most beautiful approaches to a mansion that we have seen in this country. The prevailing features in the valley that it traverses, are composed of rich hanging woods and wild rocky projections, which burst upon the eye, at various points, with mingled loveliness and grandeur not to be described by the pen. The whole is wrapped in deep seclusion; and whilst, in silence, we reverence the genius of the place, it is difficult to believe that we are, in fact, not more than five miles from the exchange of Bristol, and the busy hum of its congregated merchants!

The *Castle,* that imparts a name to this seat, is placed on a lofty and wooded eminence, which on one side impends over the precipitous face of the glen, and on the other commands enchanting views of the Severn, and a vast tract of diversified country, in which the mountains of Wales are august features. This castellated building is well designed for a prospect and banquetting house, and its principal apartment has lately been embellished in a fine taste. The Castle stands on the former site of the chapel dedicated to St. Blasius, or Blaise. In digging for its foundation many Roman coins were discovered, chiefly of brass, but some of silver. A catalogue of these is given in the Rev. Samuel Seyer's "Memoirs of Bristol," from which it appears that, they were principally coins of Vespasian, Constantine, and Gordianus. In the same work is a plan of the encampment at this place.

The discovery noticed above was not the first that had occurred, on interfering with the soil beneath the chapel of St. Blaise. In the account of Henbury, by Sir Robert Atkyns, we are told that "the foundation-stones of the chapel were dug up, in the year 1707, where many *modern coins,* as also ancient Roman coins, and other Roman Antiquities, were found. And in a vault, ten yards long and six yards broad, supposed to have been in the church, many human bodies were discovered, whose skulls and teeth were entire, white, and firm."

Many Roman coins have, also, been found, on removing the earth, in the course of extensive plantations, executed under the direction of the present Mr. Harford.

The family of Harford is of considerable antiquity in the county of Hereford. John Harford, of Bosbury in that county, Esq. who was born in the year 1504, and was son of Sir John Harford, of the same place, married Anne, daughter of Sir John Scrope, of Castle-Comb, in the county of Somerset. In an heraldic visitation, made in the reign of Henry VII., the arms of the Harfords of Bosbury are *admitted* by the Norroy king; and it may also be remarked, that, in writings of the fourteenth century, the family of Harford is styled *Antiqua et Honesta.*

In the year 1391, Richard Harford, then vicar of All Saints, Hereford, established one of the four chantries in that church, and dedicated it to the Holy Rood and St. James. Richard Harford, who was admitted B.A. in 1544, was first archdeacon of St. David's, and afterwards of Hereford. By his will he gave lands, within the town of Walton, near Tewkesbury, to Merton College, Oxford, of which society he had been a member.

In Duncumb's History of Hereford it is said that Bridstock Harford represented the city of Hereford in two parliaments, temp. Car. II. It must be observed, however, that in a work descriptive of that city by John Price, the christian name of the representative in parliament is written Peter; and it is certain that the inscription on the tomb of Bridstock Harford, M.D. (who was a man of great opulence and eminence) in the cathedral of Hereford, does not notice the supposed circumstance of his having represented the city. Peter Harford appears to have been the elder brother of that gentleman.

In the church of Bosbury are many very fine monuments to different members of this family. The extensive estates at Bosbury, formerly belonging to the Harfords, were diverted from the male line, in consequence of a family misunderstanding; and, in the year 1705, Charles Harford, Esq. representative of John Harford, of Bosbury, settled in Bristol. Edward, his son, married Elizabeth, grand-daughter of Hugh Jones, the first protestant Bishop of Llandaff; and Edward, the son of that marriage, was great grand-father of J. S. Harford, Esq. the present proprietor of Blaise Castle, who is the male representative of the Harfords of Bosbury, a family justly styled antient and honourable.—Sir Harford Jones, of Boultibrook, Bart. has affinity with this house, through a female branch, his great grandfather having married Mary, grand-daughter of Bridstock Harford, M.D. said by Duncumb to have twice represented in parliament the city of Hereford.

We have still to notice a very pleasing feature of this demesne. The grounds attached to the mansion are adorned with a lovely group of cottages, known by the name of BLAISE HAMLET. These cottages are ten in number, and were erected about the year 1810, by the late John S. Harford, Esq. father of the present proprietor, as retreats for aged persons, who had moved in respectable walks of life, but had fallen under misfortunes, preserving little, or nothing, in the shock of adversity, but unblemished character. The buildings evince no ostentation of charity, and would seem designed as elegant, though humble, places of voluntary retirement, rather than as the refuge of the needy, bestowed by the hand of neighbouring affluence. They were built after designs of Mr. Nash, and constitute a collection of practical studies in romantic cottage architecture. A terrace-walk, of a wavy outline, leads along the front of the buildings, and encloses a lawn that called for no operation of art, but was left undulating by the hand of nature. Ivy, woodbine, jessamine, and various simple flowering plants, cling to these tenements of peace, and impart to them a beautiful and appropriate dressing. As a picturesque object, this hamlet is, indeed, a gem of prodigious value to the domain. —It is a just principle, in arranging the ornamental buildings planned by the landscape-gardener, that utility should be blended with display; and hence we find, in many pleasure-grounds, that even the mimic-ruin conceals a shed, subservient to some use of pasturage or rural husbandry. How much superior are the devices here practised! since the smiling village, that adds, to the picturesque attractions of the territory, at the same time forms a memorial of the founder's exemplary benevolence.

21

Cote House

THE SEAT OF PHILIP PROTHEROE, ESQ.

THIS is one of the seats which highly adorn the country in the vicinage of Bristol, upon the north-west. It is situated in the extensive parish of Westbury-upon-Trim, near the road leading from Bristol into South Wales. The earliest information that we have been enabled to obtain, respecting this estate, bears reference to the year 1711, at which time it belonged to Mr. Saunders. In 1745, it was the property of William Phelps, Esq. who had married the widow of the former proprietor. By Mr. Phelps it was bequeathed to Sir Edward Thomas; but, in 1777, it was possessed by John Webb, Esq. M.P. for the city of Gloucester. In 1796, this estate was purchased by J. Wedgewood, Esq. of Etruria, celebrated for the high degree of excellence to which he conducted the manufacture of earthenware and porcelain. In 1806, it was sold to Sir Henry Protheroe, from whom it descended to Philip Protheroe, Esq. the present proprietor.

Cote House is a fine, spacious, and well-preserved mansion, built in the seventeenth century, but the precise date of its erection is unknown.—When we reflect on the numerous instances in which antient houses, occupying recluse situations, and constituting hereditary property, have been levelled with the ground or disfigured by serious innovations, we must view it as a remarkable, and very pleasing, circumstance, that a building like Cote House, placed near a great commercial city, and frequently changing proprietors in recent ages, should still retain its turrets and parapets, as memorials of days in which the first James, or his successor, swayed the English sceptre. Whilst in prevailing features the pile thus preserves the character of past times, the interior presents many refinements of modern taste. The paintings are not numerous, but rank amongst the best of their respective masters. The principal pictures are by Claude; Both; Wynants; and Van Os.

The lawn and pleasure-grounds, consisting of about eight acres, are disposed with great elegance. The hot-houses, which are very extensive, were erected by Mr. Wedgewood.

In the neighbourhood of this seat is found that curious natural production, the *Cotham Stone.* A coarse engraving of this species of stone is introduced, "by way of decoration," in one corner of the map prefixed to Rudder's Work on Gloucestershire. The following remarks are extracted from the " Compressed History," by Mr. Rudge. "The Cotham stone lies in a detached manner, within the surface of the ground. The upper side is full of nodules and bunches, and the prominences on some of the stones resemble the interlacings of ivy, crossing each other. They are sometimes two feet and a half long, and seven or eight inches thick. Cut longitudinally, and polished, they exhibit the appearance of landscape, trees, shrubs, and rivers."

On the authority of information obligingly conveyed by Mr. Protheroe, it may be remarked, that, within the circuit of three hundred yards, in the pleasure-grounds attached to Cote House, are found the common lime stone, the blue lias, and the red sand stone.

COTE HOUSE

Lead ore and calamine stone are found in various parts of this parish, and particularly on the estate of Pen Park, which is an object of considerable curiosity, on account of the deep and dreary cavern termed Pen-park hole, generally thought to be an exhausted lead mine.

FAIRFORD CHURCH

22

The Church of the Virgin Mary

FAIRFORD

THE Church of Fairford is beautiful as an architectural object, and is curious in having been built expressly as a receptacle for a very fine collection of stained glass, that has been justly said to form one of the boasts of Gloucestershire. This structure was erected under the auspices of the Tame family. It was commenced by John Tame, in 1493 and completed by his son, Sir Edmond, who died in 1534. The immediate cause of its erection is traditionally stated, in terms to the following effect. About the year 1492, John Tame, who was a merchant of great opulence, captured a Spanish vessel, bound from a Flemish port for Italy, and laden with stained glass.— The piety of catholic ages was a costly virtue, if cherished with much practical zeal. Happy would it have been for Christendom, if the Romish church had inculcated no doctrine less worthy, than that of religious good to the individual accruing from a munificent encouragement of ecclesiastical architecture. To the spirit thus infused by the tasteful churchmen of ages, certainly not dark as regarded the cultivation of many ornamental arts, England is indebted for those venerable piles, which are the architectural pride of the country; and to this prevailing *fashion* in religion, we must, probably, ascribe the foundation of the building under notice. Glass thus captured appeared to present an immediate appeal to the piety of the prosperous merchant; and he promptly founded a church at Fairford, for the reception of the treasure so easily obtained. He died in the year 1500, leaving to his son the task of completing the structure; and so ardent was the zeal of Sir Edmond Tame, that he appears not only to have finished this building, at a great expense, but to have erected a church on his family estate at Rendcombe.

The building constructed at Fairford, as a casket for the reception of this precious capture, or as a species of shrine for the conservation of sanctified labours in the pictorial art, is a fine specimen of the style in architecture that prevailed in the reign of the seventh Henry. It will be recollected that the florid, or highly decorated English style, then attained its greatest perfection. This mode of building, however, was attended with such prodigious labour and expense, that examples displaying the most elaborate of its characteristics, are chiefly confined to chapels, as in the instance of the Lady Chapel attached to Gloucester Cathedral, or the still more splendid edifice erected at Westminster, as a place of regal sepulture. Few parochial churches exhibit more than the broad lineaments of this gorgeous modification of English architecture; and very few are more highly embellished than that of Fairford, independent of its peculiar richness in storied glass.

This edifice is of handsome proportions, and is surmounted by a square tower, having a pierced parapet, with two crocketted pinnacles at each of its angles. The windows are broad, uniform, and enriched with much delicate tracery-work. Between the windows are graduated buttresses. An embattled parapet runs along the whole of the building, having crocketted pinnacles at equal distances. It has been observed that "the buttresses of the tower are, somewhat peculiar, as they are flattened, and gradually diminished to the top, so that, at a distance, the form appears to be octangular." Upon their bases are statues, the size of life; and in the pierced-work of the parapet are introduced many escutcheons of arms, among which occur those of Clare, Despencer, Newburgh and Tame. Round the architrave of the tower is a series of grotesque figures; and in different parts of the exterior are niches, formerly filled with statues.

The interior is divided into a nave, chancel, and two side aisles, which aisles are continued nearly to the termination of the chancel, and communicate with that part of the church by two arches of similar height. Over the nave is a clerestory, well designed for the display of illuminated glass. The finishing of every part of the interior is fine, delicate, and costly. Round the chancel is an oaken screen, excellently carved, and having ranges of stalls, ornamented in the same manner as the screen. The entire length of the church is 125 feet, and the breadth 55 feet.

The glass is disposed in twenty-eight windows, each of which has four principal compartments. In several windows the figures are now mutilated or displaced; and these instances of imperfection will cause little surprise, when it is observed that the whole of the glass was taken down, and secreted, during the civil troubles of the seventeenth century. For the liberal care thus bestowed, the public is indebted to William Oldisworth, Esq. at that time impropriator.

It is recorded by Mr. Bigland, that "a description of these windows, engrossed on vellum, was preserved in the town-chest. It is now lost; but a paper-roll, copied from it, falling into the hands of Mr. Murray, was published by Hearne, in his edition of Roper's Life of Sir Thomas More."— The subjects are chiefly scriptural, and relate to important events in the life of the Saviour, and striking passages in the Old Testament; but there are, also, representations of apostles, primitive fathers, and Roman emperors, with some allegorical devices, in the following enumeration of the principal windows, we profit by the labours of those who have described this glass, at a greater length than is consistent with the design of the present work.

"The subjects commence in the fifth window of the north aisle, on which side all the paintings are in much the best state of preservation. The third and fourth compartments of this window, which represent *Moses and the Burning Bush*, and the *Queen of Sheba offering Gifts to King Solomon*, are very finely coloured. The next window is imperfect, but commences the subjects from the History of the Redemption, which, with the exception of the Resurrection and the Day of Judgment, is concluded, in the ninth window, by a representation of the *Ascension*, and of the *Descent of the Holy Spirit*. The third window in this series is the best: in one of its compartments, displaying the *Salutation of the Virgin*, the architectural perspective of the temple is very fine. The great east window, also, of which the chief design is the *Triumphal Entry into Jerusalem*, is perfect, and extremely grand. The tenth, eleventh, and twelfth windows contain the figures of the *Twelve Apostles*. The two next windows, which represent the *Primitive Fathers of the Church*, and *King David sitting in Judgment*, are very imperfect. The designs of the great west window are the *Resurrection* and *Last Judgment*. It is observed, in 'Anecdotes of the Arts,' that 'so brilliant are the colours, and so delicate the drapery of the smaller figures, in this window, that a more pleasing specimen of antient art will rarely be found in England, or on the Continent.' The sixteenth and seventeenth windows represent the *Judgment of Solomon*; the *Evangelists*; and several subordinate subjects. The three next are adorned with the figures of *twelve prophets*. From the twenty-first to the twenty-fourth windows, inclusive, are the figures of *Roman Emperors*, and others who opposed the progress of Christianity. The remaining four are ornamented with the emperors who favoured its establishment."

The above abridged excerpt may convey general ideas of the subjects here represented; and such readers as may be desirous of obtaining more minute information, we refer to Bigland's History of this county.

In various merits of execution, and in splendour of display, this noble assemblage of stained glass is considered to be unrivalled in England, except by that which composes the windows of King's College, Cambridge. On this subject it is customary to adduce the testimony of Vandyck, who is recorded, by Hearne, to have "often affirmed to the king (Charles the First) and others, that many of the figures were so exquisitely well done, that they could not be exceeded by the best pencil." It is to be regretted that no accurate information has been obtained respecting the artists by whom the designs were made, and the work performed. A vague tradition, confidently repeated by the early historians of Gloucestershire, ascribes the former to Albert Durer; but such an ascription is evidently erroneous, as that painter was born in 1471, and was, therefore, little more than twenty years of age at the time the glass is said to have been completed, and on its passage towards Italy. Mr. Bigland, with a greater probability of correctness, conjectures that the designer might be Francesco Francia, who was born at Bologna, in 1460, and was "peculiarly eminent in the art of encaustic painting."

It is remarked by Mr. Dallaway that the best decorations in stained glass, which he could discover, on investigating Rome and other Italian cities, were those in the Convent of Santa Maria Novella, at Florence; which, in his opinion, nearly resemble those at Fairford, both in design and execution. If we had not received intelligence to this effect, from so competent a judge, we confess that we should have ventured on the boldness of conjecturing that the glass might, really, have been executed by English artists, after Cartoons probably Flemish. It will be observed that the story of the capture of this glass rests entirely on tradition; and it is well known that the glass-stainers of England had attained so great a proficiency about the close of the fifteenth century, that the magnificent works at King's College were executed by native artists, although from foreign Cartoons.

Whether the Cartoons only, or the glass in a finished state, were captured by the ship belonging to John Tame, equal veneration is due to him, as the founder of this superb structure, so truly rich in the display of various arts, honourable to the taste and abilities of the age in which he flourished. Curiosity, therefore, or a more laudable feeling, naturally prompts us to make inquiries concerning his personal fortunes, and connexion with the neighbourhood which he selected for the exercise of his munificence.

The Tames of Fairford are said by Leland to have branched from the family of that name settled at Stowel, in this county. John Tame, the founder of Fairford Church, appears to have been engaged in extensive mercantile concerns at London, where it is probable that several of his forefathers had also lived, as the name of Tame occurs more than once in the list of early sheriffs for that city. He purchased the manor of Fairford from King Henry VII. and levied a fine of the estate in the thirteenth year of that king. The great benefit he conferred on this place, by introducing the manufacture and trade of wool and clothing, is emphatically recorded by Leland, who observes that "Fairford never flourished before the coming of the Tames into it." When he retired to this town he resided in the manorial house, which was termed *Beauchamp Court*, it having been erected by the Beauchamps, earls of Warwick, who were lords of this manor for many years. The manor-house was situated near the church, and was rebuilt by himself and his son. This structure is noticed by Leland as "a fayr mansion-place of the Tames, hard by the chirche-yarde, buildid thoroughly by John Tame and Edmunde Tame; the back thereof goithe to the very bridg of Fairford."—The antient manor-house of this respectable family was taken down by Andrew Barker, Esq. who purchased the manor about the year 1670, and built a mansion, still existing, at the distance of about a quarter of a mile from the town.

John Tame died in the year 1500, and lies buried in the north aisle of Fairford Church, with Alice his wife. Over their remains is erected an altar tomb, of Italian marble, on the covering-stone of which are the effigies of the deceased, engraved in brass. Beneath the figures are the following homely lines:

For Jhus love pray for me		I may not pray—now pray ye
With a Pater Noster et an Ave	∫	That my paynys Relessed may be

At the corner of the slab are four escutcheons of arms, and round the verge is this inscription:—

Orate pro animabus Johis Tame, Armigeri, et Alicie uxoris ejus, qui quidem Joh'es obijt octavo die mensis Maij Anno Dni Millesimo quingentisimo, et anno Regis Henrici Septi sexto decimo: et predicta Alicia obijt vicesimo die mensis Decembris, Anno Dni. Milimo CCCC, Septuagesimo primo quorum a'i'abus propicietur Deus. For Jhus love pray for me: I may not pray—nowe pray ye.

The founder of the Fairford family was succeeded by his son, Sir Edmond, who thrice served the office of high sheriff for this county. He married Agnes, daughter of Sir Edward Grevil, and died in the twenty-sixth of Henry VIII. The estates of Sir Edmond devolved to his son, of the same name; who married Catherine, daughter of Sir William Dennis. He was twice high sheriff of Gloucestershire, and deceased, without issue, in 1544, leaving three sisters, co-heiresses, who married into the families of Stafford, Verney, and Watkin. The manor was purchased of those families by Sir Henry Unton and John Croke, who again sold it to the Tracys. From these proprietors it passed, by sale, to Andrew Barker, Esq. who rebuilt the mansion on a fresh site, as we have remarked in the preceding page. Samuel, the son of Andrew Barker, left two infant daughters, co-heiresses, in whom this property was vested when Sir R. Atkyns composed the History of Gloucestershire. One of these daughters died unmarried, and the survivor married James Lamb, Esq. but died without issue, in 1789. She bequeathed this estate to John Raymond, Esq. who has since, by royal sign manual, assumed the name and arms of Barker.

The benefice of Fairford is a vicarage, in the gift of the dean and chapter of Gloucester. Fairford gives the title of viscount, in the English peerage, to the Marquess of Downshire.

23

Flaxley Abbey

THE SEAT OF SIR THOMAS-CRAWLEY BOEVEY, BART.

THE seat termed Flaxley Abbey is situated in the forest division of this county, at the distance of about eleven miles from Gloucester, towards the south-west.

The Abbey of Flaxley was founded, for monks of the Cistertian order, by Roger, second Earl of Hereford. According to information conveyed by Leland, the foundation took place in consequence of a fatal accident. It appears that a brother of Earl Roger was killed by an arrow, when hunting, upon the very spot that afterwards formed the site of the religious structure. A statement to that effect was seen by Leland, inscribed on a tablet hanging in the Abbey-church. The foundation was made in the sixth year of King Stephen (1140). The monks obtained a charter, and a confirmation in their possessions, from Henry II. when Duke of Normandy; and a second confirmation was granted by the same personage, after his accession to the full powers of royalty.

By those documents it is shown that the vale in which the abbatial buildings were erected, was then termed the valley of Castiard; an appellation that has long since fallen into disuse, and is now to be found in antient writings alone. Among the possessions of the abbey is mentioned an iron work, or forge, at *Edland,* which had existed before the Norman Conquest, and has been worked, with some interruptions, to the present time. For the service of this forge a wood was granted, which remained the property of the abbot and monks at the dissolution; and it is worthy of remark that coal has not at any time been used in these iron works, the furnace and forges having been uniformly worked with charcoal, much to the benefit of the iron here manufactured. The tithes of chestnuts in the Forest of Dean were, likewise, bestowed on the monks; and the mention, in so early a charter, of large quantities of this fruit, as the produce of an English forest, may assist in strengthening the opinion, now entertained by many arborists, that the tree usually termed the Spanish Chestnut (*fagus castanea*) is, in fact, indigenous to the soil of England.

The abbey was dedicated to the Virgin Mary, and was under the jurisdiction of the Bishops of Hereford, by whom the abbots were consecrated. The annual value of the revenues was stated, at the dissolution, in the time of Henry VIII. to amount to 112*l*:3*s*:1*d*.

After the removal of the monks, the manor, together with the monastic buildings and their appurtenances, was granted to Sir William Kingston, Knt. whose descendants resided here until Anthony Kingston sold the estate, in the latter part of the seventeenth century, to Abraham Clarke, Esq. From the family of Clarke it went, by devise, to William Boevey, Esq. which gentleman died in 1692; and, after the decease of Catherine, his widow, in 1726, it passed, in pursuance of Mr. Boevey's will, to Thomas Crawley, Esq. in whose descendant, Sir Thomas-Crawley Boevey, Bart. it is now vested.

It is too often the necessity of the topographer to present mere names, when tracing the descent of property, through various hands, in successive ages. Such, in many instances, may

Flaxley Abbey

be truly said to "stand more for number than account," and act like the mutes in a pageant whilst they assist in completing the columns of manorial story. If conspicuous worth or talent be discovered, it is the duty of the writer to expatiate on it to the full extent that his limits will allow; for it is to him as a vein of precious ore, occurring in the researches of the mineralogist; and how potent a charm does the display of excellence in character, add to the attractions of that spot which he wishes to render of interest to his reader! If we would pursue our simile, borrowed from labours in mineralogy, we should say, that, in the memory of the once celebrated lady, MRS. CATHERINE BOEVEY, we have fortunately met with a vein of the purest gold; and our duty and our pleasure equally induce us to work it to the utmost.

Mrs. Boevey is mentioned, in Ballard's "Memoirs of several Ladies of Great Britain," as "a gentlewoman that was not either a linguist or a writer, but as one who was not, by any means, to be omitted in those memoirs. For as her exemplary life, and the noble use she made of an ample fortune, demanded for her an honourable place among the female worthies, so her great genius and good judgment, improved by reading the finest authors, and the wit and elegance of her conversation, which have been so much admired and celebrated by the best judges, may justly entitle her to a character amongst the learned; and if she was not a writer, may at least make us wish that she had been so."

Such were her graces of person and perfections of mind, that the tasteful authors of the Spectator alluded to this lady in their description of the WIDOW, who had raised a passion as hopeless as it was unconquerable, in the breast of SIR ROGER DE COVERLEY. This circumstance has been seldom noticed; but in a communication with which we have been favoured from Flaxley Abbey, we are assured that it is a fact well known in the family.— Mrs. Boevey was daughter of John Riches, Esq. a merchant of London, and was married, at the age of fifteen, to William Boevey, Esq. who died, as we have already remarked, in 1692; at which time his lady was in her 22nd year. She remained a widow through life, notwithstanding numerous addresses, much more urgent in reality, than was the fancied suit of the Worcestershire knight; and died January 21st, 1726, in the 57th year of her age.

The chief printed works which contain information respecting this distinguished widow, are Ballard's Memoirs; Steele's Epistolary Correspondence; and the Gentleman's Magazine for 1792. From these, and other sources, we present the following materials towards a due estimate of her character.

Sir Richard Steele dedicated to Mrs. Boevey the work termed THE LADIES' LIBRARY; and the dedication (which we here reprint) curiously exhibits the high opinion entertained of her merits, by the author who afterwards suggested so romantic and striking a literary portrait of her person and character, in some of the most pleasing pages of the Spectator.

TO MRS. BOEVEY

"It is an undisputed privilege, writers are possessed of, to produce examples to the precepts they would enforce from the living characters of their cotemporaries. You cannot, therefore, expect for ever to be doing laudable things, and for ever to escape applause. It is in vain, you find, that you have always concealed greater excellencies than others industriously present to view; for the world well know that your beauty, though in the highest degree of dignity and sweetness, is but a faint image of the spirit which inhabits the amiable form which heaven has bestowed on you. It is observable, by all who know you, that though you have an aspect and mien, which draw the attention and expectation of all who converse with you, and a wit and good sense which surmount the great conceptions of your beholders, those perfections, are enjoyed by you, like gifts of common acceptation. That lovely and affable air expresses only the humility of a great and generous heart; and the most shining accomplishments, used by others to attract vulgar admiration, are serviceable to you, only as they adorn piety and charity.

"Though your person and fortune equally raise the admiration and ambition of our whole sex, to move your attention to their importunities, your equal spirit entertains itself with ideas of a very different kind, and is solicitous to search for imperfections, where it were the utmost injustice for any other to imagine any; and applauses only awaken you to an inquisition for errours.

"It is with this turn of mind, that, instead of assemblies and conversations, books, and solitude have been your choice; and you have gone on in the study of what you should be, rather than attended to the celebration of what you are. Thus, with the charms of the fairest of your own sex, and knowledge not inferior to the more learned of ours, a closet, a bower, or some beauteous scene of rural nature, has constantly robbed the world of a lady's appearance, who never was beheld but with gladness to her visitants, nor ever admired but with pain to herself.

"But a constant distribution of large charities; a search for objects of new bounty; and a skilful choice of modest merit, or suffering virtue, touch the souls of those who partake your goodness, too deeply to be borne without enquiring for, and celebrating their benefactress. I should be loth to offend your tenderness in this particular, but I know, when I say this, the fatherless and the widow, the neglected man of merit, the wretch on the sick bed, in a word, the distressed under all forms, will, from this hint, learn to trace the kind hand which has so often, as from heaven, conveyed to them what they have asked in the anguish of soul, when none could hear, but he who has blessed you with so ample a fortune, and given you a soul to employ it in his service.

"If much more than what is here intimated be not the plain truth, it is impossible to come at what is so; since one can find none who speak of you, who are not in love with your person, or indebted to your fortune. I wish you, as the completion of humane happiness, a long continuance in being what you are."

In the New Atalantis is the following character of this excellent woman, from the pen of Mrs. Manley.—"Her person has as many charms as can be desired.—She is one of those lofty, black, and lasting beauties, that strike with reverence, and yet delight; there is no feature in her face, nor any thing in her person, her air, and manner, that could be exchanged for any others, and she not a loser. Then, as to her mind and conduct, her judgement, her sense, her steadfastness, her reading, her wit and conversation, they are admirable; so much above what is most lovely in the sex, that, shut but your eyes (and allow for the musick of her voice) your mind would be charmed as thinking yourself conversing with the most knowing, and most refined, of yours; free from levity and superficialness, her sense is solid, and perspicuous.—She is so neat, so perfect, an economist, that in taking in all the greater beauties of life, she did not disdain to stoop to the most inferior. In short, she knows all that a man can know, without despising what, as a woman, she should not be ignorant of.

"Inimitable has been her conduct, and 'tis owing to her prodigious modesty alone, that the whole empire does not sound her glory. She has desired to live unknown, and has confined herself to a narrow part of it; else her fame had been as diffusive as her merit; wisely declining all publick assemblies, she is contented to possess her soul in tranquillity and freedom at home, among the happy few she has honoured with the name of friends."

Dr. Hickes, in the Preface to his learned work, Linguarum Vett. &c. expresses his great esteem for Mrs. Boevey in elegant Latin.

In the Gentleman's Magazine for 1792, is a letter addressed to Mrs. Winstone, by Mrs. Barrow, aunt to the late Sir Charles Barrow, presenting an account of the last hours of this admired lady. After taking breakfast cheerfully with her family, on Wednesday, the 18th of January, 1726, she was suddenly seized with an internal disorder, which terminated in her decease on the following Saturday.

In the same work are given the following copies of inscriptions to her memory, on a cenotaph in the Abbey-church of Westminster, and on her funeral-monument at Flaxley.

INSCRIPTION AT WESTMINSTER.

"To the memory of Mrs. Catherine Boevey, whose person and understanding would have become the highest rank in female life, and whose vivacity would have recommended her in the best conversation; but, by judgement as well as inclination, she chose such a retirement as gave her great opportunities for reading and reflection, which she made use of to the wisest purposes of improvement in knowledge and religion. Upon other subjects she ventured far out of the common way of thinking; but in religious matters she made the Holy Scriptures, in which she was well skilled, the rule and guide of her faith and actions, esteeming it more safe to rely upon the plain word of God, than to run into any freedoms of thought upon revealed truths. The great share of time allowed to her closet was not perceived in her economy, for she had always a well ordered, and well instructed family, from the happy influence as well of her temper and conduct, as of her uniform and exemplary life. It pleased God to bless her with a considerable estate, which with a liberal hand, guided by wisdom and piety, she employed to his glory and the good of her neighbours. Her domestick expences were managed with a decency and dignity, suitable to her fortune, but with a frugality that made her income abound to all proper objects of charity; to the relief of the necessitous; the encouragement of the industrious; and the instruction of the ignorant. She distributed not only with chearfulness, but with joy, which, upon some occasions of raising and refreshing the spirit of the afflicted, she could not refrain from breaking forth into tears, flowing from a heart thoroughly affected with compassion and benevolence. Thus did many of her good works, while she lived, go up as a memorial before God; and some she left to follow her.

"She died January 21st, 1726, in the 57th year of her age, at Flaxley, her seat in Gloucestershire; and was buried there, where her name will be long remembered; and where several of her benefactions, at that place as well as others, are more particularly recorded."

UNDERNEATH, ON A WHITE MARBLE.

"This monument was erected, with the utmost respect to her memory, and justice to her character, by her executrix, Mrs. Mary Pope, who lived with her near forty years, in perfect friendship, and never once interrupted, till her much-lamented death."

INSCRIPTION AT FLAXLEY.

"In the vault near this chapel is reposited the body of Mrs. Catharine Boevey, daughter of John Riches, Esq. of London, merchant.—She was married to William Boevey, Esq. lord of the manor of Flaxley, at the age of 15, and was left a widow, without children, at the age of 22, and continued so all the rest of her life.—She entertained her friends and neighbours with a most agreeable hospitality, but always took care to have a large reserve for charity, which she bestowed not only on such occasions as offered, but studied how to employ it so, as to make it most useful and advantageous. Her disposition to do good was so well known in the district about her, that she easily became acquainted with the circumstances of those that wanted. And as she preserved many families from ruin, by reasonable loans or gifts, so she conveyed her assistance to some of the better rank, in such a manner as made it doubly acceptable. How far her bounty extended was known to herself alone; but much of it appeared, to her honour and God's glory, in frequent distributions to the poor, and especially to the charity schools round about the country; relieving those in prison, and delivering many out of it; in contributing to churches of the English establishment abroad, as well as aiding several at home; in cloathing and feeding her indigent neighbours, and in teaching their children, some of whom, every Sunday by turns, she entertained at her house, and condescended to examine them herself.—Besides this continual, it might be said this daily, course of liberality during her life, she bequeathed, at her death, towards the founding a college in the island of Bermuda, 500*l.*—To the Grey Coat Hospital in St. Margaret's; Westminster, 500*l.*—To the Blue Coat Hospital, Westminster, 200*l.*—To the Charity School of Christ's Church parish, Southwark, 400*l.*—To augment the living of this place, 1200*l.*—To put out poor children, of this parish, apprentices, the interest of 400*l.* for ever; of which sum 160*l.* had been given by Mr. Clarke and Mr. Boevey.—To be distributed as her executrix should think fit, among those whom she had put out apprentices in her life time, 400*l.*

"Lastly, she designed the re-building of this chapel, which pious design was executed by Mrs. Mary Pope."

A representation of the mansion, as it stood in the early part of the eighteenth century, whilst it constituted the residence of Mrs. Boevey, is among the engravings by Kip, illustrative of the history by Sir Robert Atkyns. The house there delineated is a fabric of considerable extent, but of low proportions, having many projecting windows in its sloping roof. In a work on the topography of this county, published a few years back, it is said that "early in the last century the ancient residence of the abbot and monks remained nearly perfect. It was low, but long in front, being sixty feet long and twenty-five feet wide. The whole was arched with stone, and the vault intersected with plain and massy ribs. The first floor contained a long gallery, and at the south end was one very spacious room, which was supposed to have been the abbot's chief room. The dormitories, or cells, were connected with the great gallery."

To this account we may add that the gardens were large, but disfigured with formal parterres, and with trees placed at uniform distances, and cut into strange shapes by those perverse horticultural artists, who flourished under Queen Anne, and who, in the language of Pope, "made it their study to recede from nature." A fanciful observer remarks to us, that, in the same view, taken during the residency of Mrs. Boevey, are to be seen two ladies, fishing, near the shade of some trees to the right of the house. These, in a page of romantic topography, would, undoubtedly, be said to represent (although poorly, it must be allowed) the widow, and that confidant, of whose influence Sir Roger so frequently complains.

A great part of the building that was thus rendered of interest by its former connexion with a monastic establishment, and by the allusions of the spectator, was accidentally destroyed by fire, on the 9th of April, 1777; and the " abbey" was re-edified, in a modern taste, under the direction of a Mr. Keck, in 1780. The building, in its present form, is a spacious and handsome residence; but, certainly, the designer neglected a fine and appropriate opportunity of introducing the characteristics of antient English architecture, in a mansion raised on the ruins of a religious house, and even retaining an abbatial appellation. In several apartments are some valuable pictures, comprising portraits by Rembrandt and Vandyck, with subjects of more general interest by Hemskerck, and other Flemish masters.

The attached grounds have experienced great improvement, since a view of this domain was engraved by Kip. The house is situated in a valley, with a fine amphitheatre of wood on each side, and a sheet of water in front. With such favourable auxiliaries of the picturesque, the territory of Flaxley wants little assistance from art. It is, indeed, predisposed to beauty; and nature would appear to smile in triumph over her escape from the shackles imposed by the barbarous rulers and lines of *artists,* who were so vain as to think that they could, with such instruments, create substitutes for her various graces. The back of the house is enclosed by a thick belt of wood, and a rich tract of meadow land. A deer-park, not large, but finely verdurous, and well stocked with deer, lies contiguous to the mansion, and affords, at several elevated points, very extensive and beautiful prospects.

In discussing the charms and deficiencies of the scenery around the various mansions in this county, we do not hesitate to submit such suggestions as may occur, towards presumed possibilities of improvement. In pursuance of such a line of conduct, we remark that the water at this place might, probably, be disposed with an increased beauty of effect; and we are confirmed in the propriety of hazarding such an opinion, by finding a similarity of thought in a tasteful and judicious correspondent. The dam-head of the large piece of water in front of the house, now crosses the view in a straight line; but, assuredly, the effect would be more pleasing, if the two extremities were concealed, as regards the view from the mansion. A bold speculator in improvements would, perhaps, propose to communicate to the plentiful water on these grounds, the aspect of a mock river, and to throw over one of its windings a handsome bridge, forming an approach to the residence.

The only remains of the antient buildings of the abbey are a few semicircular arches, at present worked into a cellar; and some traces of the church, which are now within the limits of a small garden, adjoining the house.

THORNBURY CASTLE

24

Thornbury Castle

THIS ruinous building is situated in the small town of Thornbury, at the distance of eleven miles to the north of Bristol, and twenty-four to the south-west of Gloucester.

Mr. Turner, in the first edition of the History of the Anglo-Saxons, supposes Thornbury to have been a British city, and to have constituted the residence of Cyndellan, a petty king, probably the same with the Condidan, who fell in 577, at the battle of Dyrham. No mention of Thornbury occurs in the catalogue of British towns, presented in the INTRODUCTION TO THE BEAUTIES OF ENGLAND; in forming which list the present writer was favoured with the assistance of the late Bishop of Cloyne, and Mr. Leman of Bath. It would appear, however, as is observed by Mr. Fosbroke, that this place, situated close to an antient passage of the Severn, was fortified at a very early period.

There are good reasons for believing that Thornbury was a town of some importance, in the time of the Saxons. A market was certainly established here before the Conquest; and the manor formed part of the Royal domain, at the time of the great Survey. In that record the name is written *Turneberie,* from *Torn,* or *Turne,* a court; and, within the limits of the parish, is a hamlet denominated Kington.

The manor had belonged, before the entry of the Normans, to Brictric, a Saxon thane, who had, early in life, refused the hand of Maud, afterwards queen of William the Conqueror. A very peculiar opportunity of revenge was afforded to the slighted lady, as her husband, on ascending the throne of England, bestowed upon her the estates of the man who had declined her love; and she had the barbarous gratification of effecting his utter ruin. Returning to the crown on the decease of Queen Maud, the manor of Thornbury was given, by King William Rufus, to Robert Fitz-Haymon; with whose daughter it passed, in marriage, to the family of the Earls of Gloucester. By descent from the Clares, Earls of Gloucester, through Margaret, daughter and heir of another Margaret, wife of Hugh de Audley, sister and coheir of the last Gilbert de Clare, the manor devolved to Ralph Lord Stafford, whose descendant, Humphrey Stafford, was created Duke of Buckingham.

The misfortunes which befell the dukes of this lineage, are sufficiently well known; and, indeed, a detailed account of them forms a part of national history. It must, therefore, be unnecessary for us to do more than briefly allude to the ambitious, but ill-digested, schemes which lifted Henry, Duke of Buckingham, for a short time in the reign of Richard III. to the highest pinnacle of court influence attainable by a subject, although they eventually reduced him to the circumstances of a fugitive, a culprit, and a state-victim. Duke Edward, son of that enterprising nobleman, was founder of the existing pile, termed the Castle of Thornbury; and the extensive remains of this structure are at once highly curious, as exhibiting the modes of architecture which characterised the country-seats of nobility in the time of the eighth Henry, and as memorials of a personage distinguished in the British annals, and rendered familiar to all classes of readers by the master-touches of our great dramatist.

Edward, Duke of Buckingham, it will be recollected, was one of the richest and most powerful nobles in the court of Henry VIII. His jealousy of Cardinal Wolsey is described by Shakspeare as the cause of his downfall, he having

> Heated a furnace for his foe so hot,
> That it did singe himself;

but it would appear, in fact, that he entertained schemes of ambition, more wild and dangerous than those of his father. According to depositions made at his trial, he aimed at the crown itself; and was so weak as partly to build his hopes on " a vain prophecy of Nicholas Hopkins,"

> A Chartreux friar,
> His Confessor; who fed him every minute
> With words of sovereignty.

He was charged with treason, and committed to the tower of London, on the 16th of April, 1521. His trial took place on the 13th of May following, and he was beheaded upon Tower-hill, on the 17th day of the same month. Among the reflections and adjurations ascribed by Shakespeare to his last hours, are the following, which are naturally and impressively deduced from the events that accompanied the fall of his father, as well as of himself.

> You that bear me,
> This from a dying man receive as certain;
> Where you are liberal of your loves and counsels,
> Be sure you be not loose; for those you make friends,
> And give your hearts to, when they once perceive
> The least rub in your fortunes, fall away
> Like water from ye, never found again,
> But where they mean to sink ye.

A Castle at Thornbury is noticed at the earliest period in which the place is mentioned by authentic record, and the present unfinished building occupies the site of that structure. It was commenced by the Duke of Buckingham, in the second year of Henry VIII., at which time he was high in office, and was not only the most affluent, but the most popular, nobleman of the day. The reason for his not completing the building does not appear, unless we can suppose that there was not sufficient time between the second of King Henry, and the attainder of the duke, for the performance of such an undertaking. It is known that he occasionally resided in such parts as were habitable, and it has been said that Henry VIII. passed ten days here, in the year 1539. The annalist Stowe, after noticing this building, remarks that the duke "made a faire parke hard by the Castle, and tooke much ground into it, very fruitful of corne, now faire land for coursing."

Mr. Dallaway terms the structure a "remarkable specimen of architecture, which, adopting a military appearance, displayed, likewise, the magnificence and convenience of a private dwelling;" and he bestows on it the name of a "palatial castle." This building at Thornbury; Haddon Hall, Derbyshire; and the ruinous pile of Raglan, Monmouthshire; do, in fact, present bold, extensive, and splendid examples of the *castellated house,* properly so called. It is almost unnecessary to add that this mode of design succeeded to the regular fortified dwellings of the middle ages, no example of which occurs at a later period than the reign of Richard II.

Buildings of this kind were, evidently, not designed to withstand a formal siege, but were proof against the shock of any sudden assault, however potent. They are the mute chronicles of their time; and exhibit to posterity, more clearly and decisively than the page of the historian, a portraiture of the manners that prevailed in an extinct age, very memorable and interesting in the annals of Great Britain, as it was the æra in which the genius of commerce prevailed over the spirit of chivalry, and brought in its train those sciences and arts which enrich and adorn domestic life. We find, accordingly, in this mansion, halls, bowers, and galleries which were unknown to the garrisoned dwellings erected under the early Henrys and Edwards; but we also discover that of the real elegancies of life were still entirely disregarded. The architect was not yet called upon to form galleries for the reception of paintings, nor were the charms of music summoned to any other part of the residence than the loft for minstrels in the great hall.—From an examination of the arrangements, both on the external and interior divisions of the structure, we perceive, indeed, that the manners of the age were not confirmed, but hesitated between dread and security, between rudeness and refinement.

The plan of the building, as far as it was perfected, may be thus succinctly described.—An external gateway opens into a large quadrangle, furnished with cloisters for stables, and, as some examiners have thought, with accommodations for troops in garrison. This court is commanded by a large and strong tower, on one side of which is a wall, and another gateway, that opens into a small court, communicating with the state-apartments, which are in a line, contiguous to the tower, and are distinguishable by very large and magnificent projecting windows. The chimneys are curiously constructed, and bear a great resemblance to those at Compton Wynyate, in Warwickshire. They are composed of brick, wrought into spiral columns, the bases of which are charged with the cognizances of the family, and the *Stafford knot.*

On the gatehouse is the following inscription: "This Gate was begun in the Yere of our Lorde Gode M CCCCC XI, The jj Yere of the Reyne of Kynge Henri the VII. By me Edw. duc of Bukkingha, Erlle of Harforde Stafforde ande Northamto."— To this inscription is appended the *word,* or motto, of the Duke: "Dorsnevaunt" (henceforward).

In the year 1582, a survey of these premises was taken by a jury, and the curious statement drawn up at that time has been printed in the Collectanea of Leland. The language, however, is, in many parts, now unintelligible. Our respected literary friend, the Rev. T. P. Fosbroke, has methodized this survey, and accommodated the language to the present day. From the MS. which he has obligingly handed to us, we print the following copy.

SURVEY OF THORNBURY CASTLE,
MADE IN 1582.

1.—The Base Court, containing two and a half acres, encircled with lodgings for servants. (Left unfinished.)
2.—At the entry into the castle, on the west side of the Base Court, are two gates, a large and a small one, with a wicket. On the left hand a Porter's lodge, containing three rooms, with a dungeon underneath, for a place of imprisonment (for misbehaving servants, &c.)
3.—Within was a court leading to the Great Hall, which was entered by a porch. It had, also, a passage from the Great Kitchen. In the middle of the Hall was a hearth, to hold a brazier.

At the upper end of it was a room with a chimney, called the Old Hall. From the upper end of the Great Hall a staircase ascended to the Great Chamber, at the top of which are two lodging-rooms. A room paved with brick, and chimnied, was connected with the head of the stairs. (These appear to have been lodging-rooms for visitors.)

4.—In this court, leading to the Hall, were wet and dry larders; the privy-bakehouse, and boiling-house; all communicating with the Great Kitchen. Over these apartments were lodging rooms for the servants, and above these a long loft.

5.—The Great Kitchen had two large chimneys, and one smaller. Within it was a privy-kitchen, over which was a lodging-room for the cooks.

6.—A Scullery and Pantry adjoined one side of the entry from the Kitchen to the Great Hall; the Scullery having a large flue, or chimney, in it. On the other side of the entry were two Cellars.

7.—Between these and the lower end of the hall was the Buttery; and over the whole of these last-named offices were four lodging rooms, with one adjoining room, called the Clerk's Treasury.

8.—The Chapel. (The account of this fabric is intelligible in the language of the original, and we, therefore, transcribe literally from the antient Survey.)—"From the lower end of the Great Hall is an entry, leading to the Chappel, at the corner of the end of which entry is a Sellor. The utter part of the Chappel is a fair room, for people to stand in at service-time; and over the same are two rooms, or petitions, (*sic*) with each of them a chimney, where the duke and duchess used to sit and hear service in the Chappell. The body of the Chappell itself fair built, having twenty-two settles of wainscot about the same, for priests, clerks, and quiristers."

9.—The Garden, surrounded with a cloister. Over the cloister a gallery, out of which a passage led to the Parish Church of Thornbury, having, at the end, a room with a chimney and window, looking into the church, where the duke used some times to hear service in the same church.

10.—Lodging-rooms. There were thirteen near the last-mentioned Gallery, six below, three of which had chimneys, and seven above, four of which had chimneys. These were called the *Earl of Bedford's Lodgings.*

11.—The Tower, and annexed buildings, were the immediate places of residence for the duke and duchess. They contained suites of rooms, one within another, or stories communicating by Staircases; and are thus described —The lower part of the principal building of the Castle is called the New Building. At the west end thereof is a fair tower. In this lower building (the new building, or that adjoining to the tower) is contained one great Chamber, with a chimney therein; and within that is another room with a chimney, called the Duchess's lodging. Between the last rooms was another, which formed the foundation, or lowermost part, of the Tower, with a chimney. From the lodging of the Duchess a Gallery, paved with brick, led to a staircase, which ascended to the Duke's lodging above, and was used for a privy way.— All these rooms were for the accommodation of the Duchess and her suite.

(The Survey then takes us back to the Great Hall, whence it proceeds to the Great Chamber, the Dining-room (of the family) and the Duke's lodgings. Connected with the bed-chamber of the duke, there were, for greater security, the Jewel-room and the Muniment-room. — This premised, the original language is intelligible.)

12.—"From the upper end of the Great Hall is a steyer, ascending up towards the Great Chamber, at the top whereof are two lodging-rooms. Leading from the Steyer's head to the Great Chamber, is a fair room, paved with brick, and a chimney in the same; (see No. 3, before;) at the end whereof doth meet a fair gallery, leading from the Great Chamber to the Earle of Bedford's lodging, (see No. 10;) on the one side, and to the Chappell on the other side. The Great Chamber is very fair, with a chimney therein. Within the same is one other fair chamber, called the Dining Chamber, with a chimney therein, likewise. And within that, again, is one other fair chamber, with a chimney therein also, called the Privy Chamber; and, within the same, again, is one other chamber, or closet, called the Duke's Jewel Chamber. Next unto the Privy Chamber, or the inner part thereof, is a fair round Chamber, being the second story of the Tower, called the Duke's Bed-chamber. From the Privy-Chamber a steyer leadeth up into another fair round chamber, over the Duke's Bed Chamber (like unto the same) being the third story of the tower, and so upwards, to answer a like chamber over the same, where the Evidents do lye. All of which last-recited buildings, called the *New Buildings*, are builded fair with free-stone, covered with lead."

Some remarks on the characteristics and peculiarities of this antient castellated house, are contained in Mr. Fosbroke's History of Gloucestershire; and we venture on inserting an extract of those observations, as a desirable accompaniment to his copy of the survey.

"The amoval of the dungeon to the porter's lodge, and the omission of a keep, were alterations which followed naturally from *police* superseding *war*. There appears to have been but a rere-dosse in the great hall, which was opposite to the gate-house, as usual, and the centre of communication. The ground floors were purely offices, and all above the family apartments. The hall-kitchen was for the whole household; the privy kitchen, where was the chief cook, for the lord. The garden was for exercise, after mass. One thing is, in particular, worthy of remark, and applicable to most old seats;—that from the number of passages, and the communications with the garden, hall, chapel, &c. and the division of apartments in suites, our ancestors did not generally assemble in one room (as now) particular times excepted, for meals or devotion; but resided in the same house, as separate lodgers."

It appears that, in the reign of Elizabeth, many of the principal timbers were removed from this unfinished structure. The building was fortified, in the wars of the seventeenth century, by the royalists, with a view of restraining the garrison at Gloucester. Since that time it has been gradually sinking into dilapidation, through neglect.

In concluding this brief historical sketch, we have to state, that, after the fall of Edward, Duke of Buckingham, the estate of Thornbury remained with his family until the reign of Charles I. at which time, by a marriage of the female heir, it passed to a branch of the Howard family, which obtained the title of Viscount Stafford, in the sixteenth of that king. On the decease of John Paul Stafford Howard, without issue, in 1762, the manor devolved, by family conveyances, to the Norfolk family, and is now the property of the Hon. Henry Howard, M.P.

We must, also, remind the reader, whilst contemplating the extensive ruin at this place, that, if a striking instance be wanting of the instability of human grandeur, the evanescent nature of human power, it may be found in the depth of humility into which the chief line of the Clares, Earls of Gloucester; the Bohuns, Earls of Hereford; and the Staffords, Dukes of Buckingham; sank, before it was utterly extinguished. Roger Stafford, great grandson of the mighty Edward Duke of Buckingham, was compelled, by the arbitrary government of Charles I. to surrender his claim to the barony of Stafford, because "he had no lands or means to support baronial dignity!" Jane, sister of Roger, was the wife of a *joiner*, at Newport, in Shropshire, where (writes Mr. Fosbroke) she was living, his widow, in 1637, and her son was by trade a *cobler*!

In our engraved view of the ruins of Thornbury, we show the great tower, and one part of that division of the building which contains the principal rooms. Rising in the distance, over the remains of the castellated structure, are seen the pinnacles on the tower of the parochial church.

25

Church of the Virgin Mary

THORNBURY

THE parochial church of Thornbury is in the immediate neighbourhood of the castle, and it is ascertained that a passage of communication formerly existed between the two buildings. It is generally believed, that, notwithstanding the antiquity and former extent of this place, there was no church at Thornbury before the Conquest. Such an opinion appears to have been formed chiefly on the silence of Domesday upon the subject; but it might be proved, from many instances, that this is not an infallible criterion. The question, however, is of little interest, as the present structure is, evidently, of a much later origin than the date of the Norman Conquest.

Thornbury Church is a large and handsome building, displaying, in its principal parts, the architecture of the fifteenth century. Sir R. Atkyns notices a tradition, according to which the "body of the church and the tower were built by Fitz-Harding, who dwelt at Rolls Place; and the south aisle was built by Hugh Lord Stafford." But the character of the fabric sufficiently proves the inaccuracy of such traditional ascriptions. The church consists of a nave, transept, chancel, and two aisles. Over the nave is a clerestory; and a tower rises from the western end. The windows, throughout the body of the church, are of that expansive form which characterises the luxuriant style of ecclesiastical architecture that obtained under Henry VI. and Edward IV. An embattled parapet runs round the whole of the nave and aisles. The tower is of graceful proportions, and highly decorated. Its battlements are perforated, as are also its delicate and richly-worked pinnacles.—We have mentioned, above, the tradition that ascribes the erection of this tower to Hugh, Lord Stafford. That nobleman flourished in the reign of Richard II.; and the design and ornaments of this building decidedly evince a later date in the annals of architecture. The most cursory examiner will scarcely fail to ascertain a similitude, in general character, between the tower of Thornbury, and the great central tower of Gloucester Cathedral, built about the middle of the fifteenth century.—This, indeed, may be safely pronounced one of the numerous churches that were erected during the rage of intestine warfare between the houses of York and Lancaster, at the instigation of the ecclesiastics, and, probably, intended as durable and pious efforts towards the expiation of bloodshed, and various other crimes, among the chief persons engaged in those ferocious quarrels.—The frequent introduction of the *Stafford's knot* denotes the family under whose auspices the principal parts of the building were completed.

The interior is plentifully ornamented, and in good preservation. The nave is divided from the aisles by six pointed arches and the effect of the clerestory is extremely light and pleasing. The depressed arch, indicating the approach of our national architecture to its last and florid stage, prevails in nearly all the windows to the west of the chancel. The great east window is walled up, and on the inner side are inscribed the decalogue, &c. enriched with *Grecian* ornaments!

In our account of Thornbury Castle, we have observed that a gallery formerly led from the cloister of the castle to the church, and communicated with a room, in which the Duke of

THORNBURY CHURCH

Buckingham and his family sometimes sat to hear divine service. That apartment has long since ceased to exist; but, on the outer side of the north wall of the chancel, are traces of a large arch-way; now blocked up, which, when open, was probably connected with the room noticed in the survey.

There are several monuments and funeral-inscriptions, in different parts of the church. The following are the principal persons thus commemorated. *Thomas Tyndale*, died 28th of April, 1571. *Sir John Stafford, Knt.* "gentleman pensioner, during the space of forty-seven yeares, to Queene Elizabethe and King James." This member of the Stafford family was, also, founder of an almshouse in Thornbury. He died on the 28th of September, 1624. *Jane, the wife of John Baker, Gent.* Buried 20th of October, 1640. Several lines of tender commendation conclude with the following passage: "The said John Baker hath, as his last farewell, erected (*at the place where he first brought and last left her*) this monument." *John Attwells, Gent.* died February 18th, 1729-30, who "bequeathed to this, and other parishes, for charitable uses, the sum of £1200." *Mrs. Martha Bendysh*, daughter of Sir John Bendysh, Bart. died 27th of September, 1710. The *Lady Dowager Arundel,* died 20th of June, 1744. *Colonel Beverley Robinson*, died 9th of April, 1792. *Susannah Robinson*, relict of Col. B. Robinson, "who, after a residence in this town, during her widowhood, of thirty years, died on the 22nd of November, 1822."

Sir Robert Atkyns states that "there were four chantries in this church. One dedicated to the Virgin Mary, and erected in the year 1499; another was called Barne's Chantry; the other two were Bruis Chantry, and Slymbridge Chantry, whereof the abbey of St. Austin's, in Bristol, was patron. The lands belonging to these two chantries were granted to Sir Arthur Darcie, in the seventh of Edward VI."

There are two chapels attached to the church; namely, Oldbury and Falfield. The benefice was given to the Abbey of Tewkesbury by Gilbert de Clare, and, after the dissolution of religious houses, was obtained by Christ Church College, Oxford, with which institution the patronage is at present vested.

The Ridge

26

The Ridge

THE SEAT OF EDWARD SHEPPARD, ESQ.

THIS residence is situated in the parish of Wotton-under-Edge, a neat and thriving town, distant from Gloucester nineteen miles towards the south, and four miles, in the same direction, from Dursley. The town occupies a picturesque and eligible position, at the foot of a long and lofty ridge of hilly country. The clothing manufacture is here cultivated, on a large scale; and, as the usual attendant on the successful prosecution of this lucrative branch of trade, the scenery in the vicinity of the town is enriched with villas, evincing different degrees of affluence and of taste.

The estate termed *the Ridge* was given, writes Mr. Fosbroke, "by Thomas Lord Berkeley, twentieth Henry III. to Thomas, his second son, by the name of his lands at the Edge; which Thomas dying s.p. gave them, in the thirty-first of Henry III. to Kingswood Abbey, who applied for license to obtain the fourth part of a mess. and virg. in 'La Egge,' held of themselves, by 20½d. *per ann.* from Walter Preslewe. They were included, as a member of Oselworth, in a grant to Sir Nicholas Pointz, who held them as 'two granges, called the Redge.'"

Rudder terms the Ridge "an estate, sometimes, in antient writings, dignified with the title of a manor." On the dissolution of religious houses, in the reign of Henry VIII. these lands were granted, in the manner above stated, to Sir Nicholas Pointz; and were afterwards sold, together with Oselworth, by the Pointz family, to Sir Gabriel Lowe, Knt. who certainly received suit and service for his two manors of Oselworth and the Ridge, respectively, in the reigns of Charles II., James II. and William and Mary. The estate afterwards came into the possession of the Ridler family. The daughter of Nathaniel Ridler, Esq. carried it, in marriage, to the Rev. Richard Brereton, by whom it was sold, about the year 1800. The Ridge, together with lands in the adjoining manor of Woodmancote, forming, in the whole, about 600 acres, is now the property of Mr. Edward Sheppard.

The handsome residence on this estate was erected by the present proprietor, after designs of Mr. George Repton; and is a very creditable specimen of that gentleman's talents as an architect. The situation is particularly attractive, and the house is well placed for the command of views. The home-scenery, diversified with wood and valley, is highly picturesque. The distance is vast and grand; embracing the course of the Severn, with the adjoining country, from the Malvern hills to the Bristol channel, and having the fine outline of the Welsh mountains for its boundary.

HIGHNAM COURT

27

Highnam Court

A SEAT OF SIR BERKELEY WILLIAM GUISE, BART. M.P.

HIGHNAM Court, distant two miles from the city of Gloucester, towards the north-west, is situated in the parish of Churcham. At the time of the Norman Survey, the manor of Highnam belonged to the Abbey of Gloucester; to which religious house it was given, in the early part of the eleventh century, by Wulfin Le Rue. This gift, however, did not proceed from any affection entertained by Wulfin for the monks of St. Peter's, nor from the superior motive of a zealous, but fantastical, sense of piety. In the year 1022, the secular canons had been displaced, and regular monks appointed to the abbey in their stead. This measure was productive of great discontent, particularly among the upper classes of society; and Wulfin Le Rue, meeting a party of monks on the road between Highnam and Gloucester, attacked them, and slew seven of their number. For this offence he was sentenced by the Pope to maintain, *for ever*, seven monks in Gloucester Abbey; and, as a source of support for that number of ecclesiastics, he gave his valuable manors of Churcham and Highnam. Licence to impark 80 acres in Churcham was obtained by Abbot John Thokey, in the ninth of Edward II, (1315); and, shortly after that date, the same abbot erected, at Highnam, a mansion, termed in old writings the Great Grange. It may be remarked, that, when a lease of this estate was granted by the abbey, in the year 1515, the abbot reserved a convenient part of the mansion-house, for the residence of himself and men, upon reasonable summons, when the plague should be in Gloucester, and as long as it should continue there."

At the dissolution of monasteries the manor was granted to John Arnold, who held a lease of this property from the Abbey, at the annual rent of £20. With the Arnold family the estate remained through several descents, and was then carried in marriage, by a daughter and heir, to Sir Thomas Lucy, of Charlecot, in Warwickshire. Dorothy, the daughter and heir of Sir Thomas Lucy, married Sir William Cooke, who died seized of this manor in 1618. He was succeeded by his son, Sir Robert Cooke; and the family remained possessed of this estate through many descents. William Cooke, of Highnam, an officer of some distinction, on the side of the parliament, in the civil wars, served the office of high sheriff in 1663, and represented the city of Gloucester in several parliaments. William Cooke, Esq. grandson of the above-mentioned William, also sat 'in parliament' for Gloucester. This last-named gentleman left two daughters, his coheirs; Anne, married to Roynon Jones, and Mary to Henry Guise, whose son, Sir John purchased the moiety of the Jones family. The manor of Highnam, together with the contiguous manors of Over and Linton, also situated in the parish of Churcham, is now the property of Sir Berkeley William Guise, Bart. M.P. for the county of Gloucester.

The antient mansion of Highnam, which we have already said was designed as a grange for the abbey of Gloucester, and was erected by Abbot Thokey, shortly after the year 1315, was the scene of several conflicts in the civil wars of the seventeenth century. After being successively garrisoned by both parties, it was, at length, rendered uninhabitable by fire. The most memorable transaction of those disturbed times, in which Highnam is concerned was the capture of a considerable body of Welchmen, who had posted themselves in the mansion at this place, and commenced intrenchments, with other preparations for regular defence. The inhabitants of Gloucester encouraged, for many ages, a sort of *border* hatred towards the Welch; and the vicinity of these foes, who are stated to have been more than 1500 in number, was viewed by them as an intolerable grievance. Sir William Waller, at the head of some veteran troops on the parliamentarian side, advanced from Wiltshire to their relief. The events which followed are minutely recorded by Corbet, in his "Military Government of the city of Gloucester."

It appears from this writer that Waller "gave notice of his advance unto L. Colonell Massie, with directions instantly to draw forth both horse and foot, before Highnam, and keepe them (the Welch) in continuall action, that they might not understand his approach. He gave order, likewise, that those flat bottomes which were brought from London, upon carriages, for service upon the river Seaverne, should be sent downe to Framilode passage, six miles below Gloucester, where both horse and foot were arrived by noone, passed over the river before night, and, unawares of the enemy, got between them and home, tooke them in a snare, and intercepted their flight. The governour performed according to the intention of the plot, drew forth all the horse, and a party of 500 foot, brought up the ordnance neere the house, and kept them in the heate of play till the evening. At night he set guards round the house, with that straitnesse and confidence that the enemy durst not stirre, nor a spy steale out, although they lay 1500 strong. At sunne-rising they had a fresh alarme by our ordnance, and were held to it by our musket shot. This morning their horse issued out, attempting to force their way through the horse guard," which they effected, but were beaten back by the infantry. "In this point of action, Sir W. Waller came up, and shot his warning peece on the other side, which dasht the enemy, and so revived our men that they ran up with fury, stormed a redoubt, and tooke in it two captaines, and above thirty private souldiers; which service had a maine influence upon the surrender of the house. Sir William placed his army to the best advantage for show, and displaid the colours of two foot regiments, reduced to 150 men, drew neere the house, and made some few shot with his canon. After his approach not a man of the enemy was slaine or hurt, yet the common souldiers would doe any thing but fight, when they were well fortified and had a sufficient magazine." On the following day the blockaded garrison yielded themselves prisoners, on condition that "the officers should receive respect and quarter, according to their quality." Sir W. Waller states the number of persons captured on this occasion, to have been 1444 "common prisoners, well-armed; and commanders and gentlemen about one hundred and fifty."

During the siege of Gloucester a skirmish took place, "in a broad lane near Highnam house," in which a captain, and four common soldiers, on the side of the royalists, were slain.

The present mansion is a spacious and substantial fabric, erected as speedily after the destruction of the antient house, as was rendered practicable by the restoration of tranquillity, and, probably under the auspices of William Cooke, who had acted as a colonel, on the side of the Parliament, in the Civil war but was received into favour by Charles I. and served, in the year 1663, the office of high sheriff of Gloucestershire. It is conjectured by Mr. Dallaway that the design was furnished by Carter, a pupil of Inigo Jones; and the Editors of the Beauties of England remark a similitude between this mansion and Coleshill-house, in Berkshire, a building evincing nearly the latest style of Inigo.

Highnam displays, externally, few graces of domestic architecture. The roof of the house is shewn, with numerous projecting attic windows; a fashion borrowed from the French architecture of the seventeenth century, but which was discarded in the buildings last designed by Jones.

The interior presents many fine and spacious apartments. In regard to interior arrangement, and ornament, much scope for originality of design was open to Inigo Jones and his followers. The great alteration of manners which took place in the last half of the seventeenth century, rendered undesirable and obsolete the long galleries, and vast halls, of the mansions which briefly succeeded to the use of castellated structures. The visiters were no longer provided with distinct suites of rooms; and the family, with their friends, assembled, with augmented confidence and familiarity, in rooms appropriated to breakfast, dinner, and the stately *circle* of evening conversation. The architect, therefore, whilst making a suitable-arrangement, bestowed a novel richness of decoration on apartments intending to display the increased urbanity of family manners. The fashion introduced was that of weightily-stuccoed ceilings, heavy cornices, and an abundance of ornamental carving. Such are the invariable characteristics of the most costly domestic buildings of this era, when preserved free from innovation.

A portrait of William Cooke, Esq. under whose direction the existing mansion of Highnam Court appears to have been erected, and who was, for some time, a zealous adherent of the parliamentarian party, has been engraved, from a drawing in the possession of Sir B. W. Guise, and now at Rendcombe, as a frontispiece to the second part of "Bibliotheca Gloucestrensis." It is inscribed "The Bannerol and Device of Colonel William Cooke, of Highnam Court, borne 1643." On this "bannerol" the colonel is represented in armour. In his left hand he holds a cocked, or triangular, hat; and he is portrayed in the act of cutting away, with his sword, the angles of this discarded badge of the cavaliers, indicative of his assuming thoroughly the party and character of a *roundhead*. Over the figure is a scroll, bearing this inscription: MUTO QUADRATA ROTUNDIS.

In the principal rooms of Highnam are several portraits and cabinet pictures, of considerable interest. It is well known that Brigadier General Guise bequeathed to Christ Church College, Oxford, in 1765, the very large collection of paintings which he had formed during his residence in Italy. The family pictures, however, were returned to the heir-at-law. We notice, in this place, some of the best and most interesting paintings in the possession of Sir B. W. Guise, both at this seat and at Rendcombe.

AT HIGHNAM COURT.

Descent from the Cross. Jordaens.
Nathan and David. Annibal Caracci.
Ecce Homo. Canavagio.
View of Venice. Canaletti.
Duchess of Cleveland. Sir P. Lely.
Brigadier General Guise. Hamilton.

AT RENDCOMBE.

Virgin, and Child sleeping. Guido.
St. Cecilia (small). Raphael.
St. Sebastian. Spagnoletti.
A Magdalen. Carlo Dolce.
Christ bearing the Cross. Ludovico Caracci.
The Vision of St. Francis. A carton. Murillo.
Infant Christ. The same.
A Cook's Shop. Snyders.

Two pictures of a Spanish Guard-room, in the Duke of Alva's wars. Teniers.

A Fruit Girl, with two roguish Boys. Velasquez.

Spanish Horses and Dogs. The same.

Eggs, Vegetables, &c. The same.

Portrait of Oliver Cromwell. Walker. This original portrait was given by Oliver himself to Colonel Cooke, of Highnam.

Algernon Sidney. Sir Peter Lely.

Mrs. Lane, who conducted the escape of Charles II. after the battle of Worcester. The same.

Sir John Guise, and Mrs. Barrington, his daughter. Sir J. Reynolds.

The park attached to Highnam Court is of considerable extent, and derives a great increase of beauty from a fine sheet of water, which, probably, formed an attraction beyond the value of the picturesque, in the esteem of the good abbot of Gloucester, when he selected the site of this mansion as a suitable spot for occasional ecclesiastical retirement.

28

Prinknash Park

THE SEAT OF THOMAS JONES HOWELL, ESQ.

PRINKNASH is an extra-parochial district, adjoining Upton St. Leonard's, at the distance of about four miles from Gloucester, towards the south-east. This is an antient manor of the abbey of St. Peter, Gloucester; and here the abbot had a country residence, surrounded by an imparked demesne. Licence of free warren, on the lands of Prinknash, was granted to the abbey by King Edward III. in 1355; which licence was confirmed by Richard II.

After the dissolution of religious houses, this manor was granted (May 14th, thirty-sixth of Henry VIII.) to Edward Bridges and Dorothy Praye. It subsequently passed through the families of Sandys, Scudamore, Chaloner, and Bridgeman. Sir John Bridgeman, who possessed this estate soon after the third of James I. was chief justice of Chester, and was descended, according to Atkyns, from an antient family of that name, which long resided at Littledean, in this county. John Bridgeman, Esq. was lord of this manor at the beginning of the eighteenth century, and was followed, in possession of the property, by Henry Toye Bridgeman, Esq. It may not be superfluous to remark, that Mr. Fosbroke informs us he had authority for believing, in regard to this last-named proprietor, that a Mr. Toye was merely named in the will of Mr. Bridgeman, as a remainder-man, or contingent successor. The whole of the other persons named in that will died, however, before the gentleman thus stationed in what may be termed the forlorn hope. He, accordingly, succeeded to the estate, and assumed the name of Bridgeman. In 1770, the property was purchased of Henry Toye Bridgeman, Esq. by John Howell, Esq.; who, dying in 1802, was succeeded by his son, Thomas Bayley Howell, Esq. father of Thomas Jones Howell, Esq. judge advocate of the forces, and judge of the vice admiralty court at Gibraltar, who is the present proprietor. The two gentlemen last named are known, and respected, by the public, as successive editors of the State Trials.

The present mansion of Prinknash is the antient building of the Abbots of Gloucester, altered in many respects, but retaining some of the exterior, and much of the internal arrangement, of the days in which those affluent ecclesastics here enjoyed a hospitable relaxation from the formalities of cloistered dignity. The situation is exquisitely fine; and the choice of a site so truly beautiful, reflects no trivial a degree of credit on the taste of the churchmen by whom it was made. The house stands on the acclivity of a lofty and wooded hill, commanding prospects, delightfully various, over a tract of country scarcely to be exceeded for richness in the midland districts. The city of Gloucester, magnificent in its pile of cathedral architecture, forms a prominent feature in this noble expanse of scenery, when viewed from several parts of the domain.

Mr. Fosbroke observes that "this is the finest remain of the abbatial residences of Gloucester, and in high preservation. Abbot Malvern (abbot from 1514 to the dissolution) is said to have rebuilt, or repaired, the house; but the great Hall is of the time of Edward IV. having, in the centre of one of the beams, a large falcon, and fetter-lock *open*; a device of that king. The opening of the lock denotes

PRINKNASH PARK

that the obstruction of the house of York to the throne was removed. Henry VIII. and his Queen, Jane Seymour, slept here; and, according to custom, their arms were placed, in stained glass, in the windows of the great chamber, as are also several other coats, of proprietors of the mansion."

In the correspondence of Horace Walpole, (Earl of Orford) with Mr. Cole, are some particulars concerning a visit to this seat, which may not be unacceptable in the present page. Mr. Walpole dates from Matson, August 15th, 1774, and thus writes of Prinknash. "Yesterday I made a jaunt four miles hence, that pleased me exceedingly, to Prinknash, the individual villa of the abbots of Gloucester. It stands on a glorious, but impracticable, hill, in the midst of a little forest of beech, and commanding elysium. The house is small, but has good rooms; and, though modernized here and there, not extravagantly. On the ceiling of the hall is Edward the Fourth's jovial device. The chapel is low and small, but antique, with painted glass, with many angels in their coronation robes, *i.e.* wings and crowns." After observing that Henry VIII. once slept here, Mr. Walpole says "under a window is a barbarous bas-relief head of Harry, young: as it is still on a sign of an alehouse, on the descent of the hill."

The favourite cognizance of Edward IV., to which Lord Orford alludes, in the above extract, is carved within a rose, on the ceiling of the hall. In addition to the remarks already presented, it may be desirable to give, in further explanation of this device, the following passages from the Heraldic Inquiries of Mr. Dallaway. "The falcon, on the fetterlock, was the device of his (Edward IV.) great grandfather, Edmund of Langley, first Duke of York, fifth son to King Edward the Third, who, after the king, his father, had endowed him with the castle of Fotheringhey, which he new built, in form and fashion of a fetterlock, assumed to himself his father's falcon, and placed it on a fetterlock; implying, thereby, that he was locked up from the hope and possibility of the kingdom. Upon a time, finding his sons beholding this device set upon a window, he asked what was latin for a fetterlock? whereupon the father said if you cannot tell me, I will tell you, 'Hic, hæc, hoc, taceatis,' revealing to them his meaning, and advising them to be silent and quiet, as God knoweth what may come to pass. This his great grand child, Edward the Fourth, reported, and bore it, and commanded that his younger son, (Richard) Duke of York, should use the device of a fetterlock, but opened, as Roger Wall, a herald of that time, reporteth."

"The cognizances," says Mr. Dallaway, "of the brothers of the house of York, Edward and Richard, are very frequently alluded to by Shakspeare, in his historical dramas;

'Made glorious summer by this *Sun* of York.'

But his (Edward's) favourite cognizance was the falcon and fetterlock, with an equivocal motto, which Mr. Walpole observes, 'had not even delicacy to excuse the witticism.'"

Besides the painted glass noticed by Lord Orford, there are, well preserved in a window, of the drawing-room, the armorial bearings, surmounted by the mitre, of Parker, the last abbot of the monastery of St. Peter, Gloucester. There are, also, many other heraldic devices, in different parts of the building; and Mr Howell has in his possession much painted, or stained, glass, in a mutilated condition, which was, probably, taken from the antient windows, when they were removed to give place to modern sashes. On one of these is painted the mitre of an abbot, with the initial letters W. M. A. M. and the words Mersos Reatu; which words appear to have formed part of a motto, used by the abbot to whose mitre they are attached. The same words appear on other pieces of this mutilated glass.

We have much pleasure in observing that Mr. Howell has lately done away with two offensive modern sashes, in one of the wings of the west front, and has restored windows consonant to the architectural character of this interesting building. In these windows he has, likewise, tastefully inserted antient painted glass. The present proprietor has, also, greatly improved the grounds, by plantations, and many touches of alteration in disposal, which bestow on them more the appearance of an imparked demesne than they had worn, in recent years, previous to the date of his acceding to the property. Mr. Howell possessed a considerable estate, in the contiguous parishes of Upton St. Leonard's, and Matson.

Thomas Jones Howell, Esq. to whom Prinknash is indebted for the above pleasing improvements, is, in right of his mother, one of the coheirs of the antient barony in fee of Zouche of Haringworth, created by writ of summons in the year 1308. This barony fell into abeyance in the year 1625, when Edward, the eleventh baron, died, leaving two daughters, coheirs of the title. Sir Cecil Bisshopp, of Parham Park, in the county of Sussex, Bart. having petitioned his late majesty, King George III. as one of the coheirs to the barony of Zouche of Haringworth, and the proofs of his pedigree being referred to a committee of privileges of the House of Lords, it was resolved, 24th of April, 1807, "that the said barony is in abeyance between Sir Cecil Bisshopp, and Mrs. Oliver, Mrs. Hemming, and Mrs. Howell, as co-representatives of the eldest daughter of the last Lord Zouche, who died in 1625, and the descendants, if any exist, of Mary Zouche, his youngest daughter."

The barony remained in abeyance until July 27, 1815, when, in the exercise of the royal prerogative, his Royal Highness the Prince Regent, in the name, and on the behalf, of his Majesty, was graciously pleased to "order a writ to be issued, under the great seal of the united kingdom of Great Britain and Ireland, for summoning Sir Cecil Bipshopp, of Parham Park, in the county of Sussex, Baronet, up to the House of Peers, by the name, style, and title of Baron Zouche, of Haryngworth, he being lineally descended from the eldest of the two daughters of Edward, the last Lord Zouche, of Haryngworth, who died, without issue male, in 1625, and *one of the rightful heirs of the said barony.*"

It would appear, from expressions in the grant of Prinknash by Henry VIII. to Edward Bridges and Dorothy Praye, that the grounds attached to this seat formerly contained a vineyard. It should also be recorded that King Charles I. was entertained here, during part of the time that the besieging army lay before Gloucester.

29

Hempstead

THE RESIDENCE OF LORD JOHN-THOMAS-HENRY SOMERSET

THIS residence is distant about one mile from the City of Gloucester, towards the south-west, and presents a pleasing object, when viewed, through its fine and venerable avenue of trees, from the road leading between Gloucester and Bristol. The house is seated on elevated ground, and commands good views over the city and contiguous country.

It is stated, in Domesday, that the manor (termed in that record *Hechanestede*) had been held under the Saxon government, by Edric the long, or long-handed, "a thane of Earl Harold's." It was afterwards held by Earl William, in demesne; but at the time of compiling Domesday, was let by the sheriff, at 60*s.* yearly rent.

In the next century this manor formed part of the great possessions of Milo, Earl of Hereford, who, in the year 1136, bestowed it on the neighbouring priory of Lanthony, a house founded by himself. After the suppression of that house, the manor was granted to Thomas Atkyns and Margaret his wife, from whom it descended to Sir Robert Atkyns, of Saperton, the historian of this county. On the dispersion of Sir Robert's property, after his decease, the manor of Hempstead was purchased by the family of Lysons, who had previously possessed a house and estate in the parish. Two learned members of this family have distinguished themselves by antiquarian and topographical writings: the Rev. Daniel Lysons, M. A. F. R. S. &c.; and the late Samuel Lysons, F. R. S. and Director of the Antiquarian Society. The handsome mansion, of which we present an engraved view, was erected by the former of these gentlemen, and is now occupied by Lord John-Thomas-Henry Somerset, younger brother of his Grace the Duke of Beaufort.

HEMPSTEAD

30

Duntesbourne Abbots

THE SEAT OF WILLIAM HUNTER BAILLIE, ESQ.

THE manor of Duntesbourne, said to consist of five hides, was given to the Abbey of St. Peter, Gloucester, in 1085, by Emmeline, wife of Walter de Lacy, for the good of her husband's soul. Previously to this grant, Walter de Lacy had bestowed on the abbey one villain; and, in the year 1100, Gilbert de Eskecot, with his wife, and his son Robert, gave to the same monastery all their lands in this manor. On the dissolution of monastic houses, the estate was granted to William Morgan and James Dolle. Oliver Dolle, Gent. was seated here in 1682-3; at which time he was summoned hence by the heralds. At a subsequent date, which we cannot precisely ascertain, the Pleydell family, who had before purchased estates in this parish, also bought the manor. Harriot, daughter and sole heir of Sir Mark Stuart Pleydell, carried the manor to William Viscount Folkstone; and by her descendant, the late Earl of Radnor, it was sold to Thomas Raikes, Esq. By that gentleman it was resold to the late Matthew Baillie, M.D.; and is now the property of his son, William Hunter Baillie, Esq.

Duntesbourne Abbots is situated about five miles from Cirencester, towards the north-west. A small *bourn*, or brook, rises in this parish, and joins the Churn at Cirencester. The Ermyn Street passes along its borders, upon the north-east. The house is not large, and is chiefly remarkable for the beautiful scenery afforded by the neighbourhood. Matthew Baillie, M.D. whose name has added some interest to this seat, was son of the Rev. James Baillie, professor of divinity at Glasgow, and was initiated in professional knowledge by his maternal uncles, the late Dr. William and Mr. John Hunter. He took his degrees at Oxford, and was admitted M.D. in 1798. Attaining great medical eminence, he was appointed physician to the late king. Dr. Baillie was author of a work, of established credit, entitled "The Morbid Anatomy of the Human Body," and other writings on subjects connected with his professional researches. His family is, indeed, distinguished for talent in literary composition. A far-distant age will acknowledge the great powers in dramatic writing possessed by his celebrated sister, Miss Joanna Baillie. We hope that we do not exceed the just bounds of commendation, when we say that this lady partakes more of Shakspeare's cast of genius, than any other dramatist, of any age or country. It may not be altogether irrelevant, or intrusive, to mention that the present writer drew up some "Remarks on the Genius of Miss Baillie," which were first published in the Universal Magazine for August, 1810.

Dr. Baillie married a daughter of Dr. Penman, and sister of the eminent barrister, now M.P. for Nottingham. He died at this seat, in the year 1823.

Whilst engaged in noticing an estate in the VICINITY OF CIRENCESTER, we find it expedient to advert to another parish in this neighbourhood, for the purpose of introducing some particulars of information that may be useful to a future, and more regular, historian. The parish to which we allude is that of SOUTH CERNEY, situated on the river Churn, at the distance of four miles

DUNTESBOURNE ABBOTS

from Cirencester.—A moiety of a manor in this parish, called *Wye's*, or *Gower's, manor*, to which some property in the parish of Minety was annexed, was purchased by John Jones, Esq. in the year 1677. After the decease of that gentleman it descended to his eldest son, Thomas, who served the office of high sheriff of this county, and, in 1740, bought the other moiety of the manor. He was succeeded in this estate by his eldest son, John, who, in the year 1764, purchased one third part of the principal manor in the same parish, called *Sir Robert Atkyns's manor*. The whole of the property mentioned above, together with a considerable landed estate, and some houses, in S. Cerney, is now possessed by Thomas Jones, Esq.

CHEVENAGE HOUSE

31

Chevenage House

THE RESIDENCE OF JOHN DELAFIELD PHELPS, ESQ.

THE antient and fine mansion of Chevenage is situated in the parish of Horsley, at the distance of about one mile and a half from the town of Tetbury. This is a delightful tract of country, and partakes in character with that which we have described in the vicinity of Spring Park, and Gatcombe. It consists chiefly of hills, often shaded by rich masses of beech wood, and lovely narrow vales, along whose verdant bosoms many rivulets glide. The acclivities are sometimes steep, and the wavy hills have nothing of formality in their disposal, but present, in their numerous combinations, examples of the picturesque, greatly dissimilar each from the other, and charming in every variety. This may, indeed, be styled a romantic region. The poetical and pictorial visiter will, perhaps, regret that scenes so congenial to their tastes are not left in the dignity of solitude, or, at most, free from any other interruption than the venerable manor-house, or rural tenement, fraught with tales of the *olden time*, or wearing the semblance of peace and simplicity. The civil economist, however, less pleasing but more useful in his views and considerations, will be gratified to find that the rivulets which steal through these sweet vales, are made conducive to the employment of a busy population, engaged in the clothing manufacture. This trade, so favourable to the prosperity of Gloucestershire, will, assuredly, be thought, by most examiners, to animate agreeably, rather than to oppress or disfigure, the face of the country. The mills, and other extensive works, in several parts of the large parish of Horsley, are objects of curiosity and interest that make ample atonement, in the esteem of all but a few, for some slight infringements on the purity of the picturesque.

The manor of Horsley had belonged, before the Conquest, to Goda, sister of Edward the Confessor, and was given by King William I. to Roger de Montgomery, who bestowed it on the monks of Troarn, in Normandy. In the reign of Edward I. the monks of Troarn conveyed it to the priory of Bruton, in Somersetshire, in exchange for the manor of Lion, in Normandy; and it remained with that religious house until the dissolution, when it was granted (A.D. 1542), to Sir Thomas Seymour. On the attainder of Sir Thomas, in 1553, it was regranted to Sir Walter Dennis, of Dyrham; by whose son, Richard Dennis, Esq. of Siston, it was sold to the family of Stephens. Henry Stephens, Esq. dying shortly before the year 1800, without male issue devised this estate to Henry Willis, Esq. who assumed the name of Stephens. Mr. Willis was descended, in the female line, from Richard Stephens, of Eastington; and on his decease, at Paris, he bequeathed it to his nephew, Henry Richmond Shute, Esq. who died in December, 1823. Under a limitation, as we believe, in a deed made by her uncle, the late Henry-Willis Stephens, Esq. this property is to come into the possession of Miss Shute, sister of Mr. H. R. Shute, deceased, when she shall attain the age of twenty-five years; a period not yet arrived. The mansion is now occupied by John Delafield Phelps, Esq.

Chevenage House is a fine and venerable pile, erected, in the reign of Elizabeth; and the buildings are disposed in the form of the letter E, in compliment to that queen. On the porch is the date of 1579. The house experienced some alterations from the late Henry Stephens, Esq.; but these are, in general, executed with so much correctness of taste, that they may be termed improvements. As usual, in mansions, which, from the date of their erection, are frequently called *Elizabethan,* the chief attention of the architect, in regard to the interior, was bestowed on the hall. This is a noble and lofty apartment, with a gallery for music. In the large windows is much stained glass consisting of the arms of the Empire of Germany, the Stafford knot, and other heraldic devices. The walls are covered with objects of considerable interest or curiosity. Among these are several suits of armour, and antient offensive arms, of various ages, together with a fine series of family portraits, including a valuable original of Robert Dudley, Earl of Leicester, the favourite of Elizabeth. In three of the bed-rooms is some good and well-preserved tapestry, representing passages in the Adventures of Don Quixotte. There are, also, two very antient and magnificent bedsteads.

The Drawing-room has silk hangings, purchased at the sale of Mr. Beckford's gorgeous collection of furniture and rarities.

Adjoining the mansion is a family-chapel. To this building was removed, with great care, about the year 1803, the gateway of a structure near Horsley Church, which had constituted a cell to the priory of Bruton. In the excellent gardens attached to this house is a fir tree, of unusual size and beauty. It is more than a century old, and is as curious, and, in its way, as superb a natural production, as the celebrated laurel at Piercefield.

The character of country which we have described as prevailing through the greater part of the parish of Horsley, is not strictly applicable to the situation of Chevenage-house, which building is seated upon a tract of rich meadows, among the Cotswold arables. A good view of Tetbury is here obtained, and the place likewise commands extensive and fine prospects over an undulating part of Wiltshire.

In the close neighbourhood of the house are the church, and decayed castle, of Beverstone. The ruins are not picturesque, and present the traces of a square building, having a tower at each angle. This was a fortified residence of the Berkeley family, and was rebuilt by Thomas, Lord Berkeley, with the money he had acquired, in ransom for prisoners taken at Poitou. It was besieged, and surrendered to parliament, in 1643. Little that is ornamental of the fabric now remains, to impart a grace and an interest to the tales of past days:

> Inexorably calm, with silent pace,
> Here Time has past:—What ruin marks his way!

The antient British trackway, or road, termed Akeman Street, runs across Chevenage Green, in its course from Cirencester to Aust, or Oldbury.

Several persons, known to the public as authors, were born in this parish. The most distinguished of these memorable natives is a living writer, the Rev. T. P. Fosbroke. This gentleman's "History of Gloucestershire," "British Monachism," and "Encyclopedia of Antiquities," will be lasting evidences of his talents and industry, in antiquarian and topographical inquiries. We hope that we are not trespassing too far on the delicacy of private feelings, when we add that his worth, as a man and a divine, demand, in this literary and enlightened age, that patronage of his zeal as a clergyman, which may atone for inevitable deficiencies in a solid remuneration of his labours, as an author.

32

Berkeley Castle

THE SEAT OF COLONEL WILLIAM FITZHARDINGE BERKELEY

THIS interesting monument of the rude splendour that marked the feudal ages, is situated in the immediate vicinity of the town of Berkeley, in the south-western part of the county, but is not remarkable for the beauty of its site, as are (perhaps fortuitously) the castle of Warwick, and several other buildings, originally intended chiefly as places of defence. Nor are its massy towers, and extensive ranges of embattled building, productive of that picturesque effect of architectural display which we witness in many fortified piles of the middle ages. It is, however, extremely curious in having experienced few alterations of importance, since the days in which its ramparts were trodden by warriors encased in steel; and this freedom from essential innovation is unusually gratifying to the feelings of the examiner, as the buildings, thus venerable in the untouched aspect of antiquity, stand connected with many memorable passages in national annals.

Roger Berkeley, whose principal residence was at Dursley, received this place from King Edward the Confessor, to whom he was related. On his death, without issue, the estate was possessed by William, his nephew and heir, whose son, named Roger, was a partizan of Stephen; and, in consequence of taking that side in politics, was deprived of his estate, which King Henry II. bestowed on Robert Fitzharding, ancestor of the present family of Berkeley, in whose posterity (with the exception of temporary alienations to the crown) the honours and estate have ever since remained.

There is some difficulty in ascertaining the exact period at which the existing castellated buildings were commenced. It is said that Roger Berkeley had a castle here, in the time of the Confessor; but we cannot perceive any architectural reasons for believing that parts of the present pile are of an Anglo-Saxon original, and are of opinion that the most antient divisions were erected near the close of the eleventh, or early in the twelfth century. Large additions were made at various subsequent periods; and, although no information completely satisfactory can be obtained, in regard to these augmentations, some useful hints of intelligence are afforded by different historians, which we collect in this place, as materials towards a critical examination of this curious baronial residence.

We are told by Atkyns, that Robert Fitzharding, the first of this family that possessed the honours of Berkeley, "repaired and enlarged the castle." This Robert lived in the reign of Henry II. In a transcript from Smythe, inserted in the collections towards a history of Gloucestershire, by Mr. Fosbroke, it is said that Maurice, son of the above-mentioned Robert, and two of his successors in the reigns of Edward II. and III. erected the two outer gates, and all the buildings within them. This assertion, however, is not readily understood; for, if the writer by the term gates meant merely fortified gateways, there are, in the present state of the building, no more than two. It is worthy of observation, that Maurice, the son of Robert thus noticed as founder of many additional parts of the castle, was the first of the Fitzhardings that dwelt at Berkeley,

BERKELEY CASTLE

from which place he assumed a name. By Sir R. Atkyns, deriving his intelligence from Smythe, it is said; that this Maurice, "fortified the castle;" by which term, we are to understand, that he obtained the royal license for that purpose. He died in 1189, the first year of Richard I.

Such are the statements afforded by local historians, and they are satisfactorily corroborated by an investigation of the buildings, which may be reasonably thought to bear internal testimony of the dates thus ascribed to them; namely, that the keep, evidently the most antient part, was probably erected soon after the year 1091, by William de Berkeley, nephew and heir of Roger, the first lord of that name; and the long ranges of additional buildings, for the increasing purposes of state, and the accommodation of the family and their retainers, were perfected at various subsequent periods, but chiefly in the fourteenth century.

Before we enter on a descriptive outline of intelligence respecting the castle-buildings, it must be desirable to take a brief review of the principal historical events connected with them. Without such reminiscences the pile, in its utmost pride of old English grandeur, affords to all, except the professed architect and antiquary, merely the contemplation of a prodigious mass of embattled masonry, cold, gloomy, and repulsive. With the inspiriting impulse of such recollections, every tower and rampart become peopled in the fancy with the actors of gaudy or tragic pageants in other days, congenial in character with the harsh dignity of the edifice.

The confederated barons, in the time of King John, had many meetings here; Robert Lord Berkeley, then proprietor of the castle, being one of the most active of the nobles that obtained the great charter from the crown. King John was, also, himself at Berkeley, on the 19th of August, 1216, the last year of his reign

It is recorded that King Henry III. twice visited this castle and "lodged here several nights." Some ideas respecting the festive pomp that prevailed at these regal visits, may be gathered from a notice of the family establishment; which, about this time, is known to have consisted, besides husbandmen employed on the demesne, of two hundred attendants, under the denominations of knights, esquires, yeomen, grooms, and pages. The wages of an esquire were then 3½d. a day, with the allowance of a horse and two suits of furred clothes, and 1½d. a day, for a boy to wait on him.

The next approach of royalty to these towers was in gloom and terror, and the regal visitant never repassed the portal, until the portcullis was raised to allow egress to his corpse. It is well known that the grandson of Henry III. the weak and misguided Edward II. expired within these walls. As if history we're not sufficiently copious on a theme so mournful, poetry has blazoned forth this transaction, in a strain calculated for lasting popularity. The lines of Gray are familiar with most readers:

> "Mark the year, and mark the night,
> When Severn shall re-echo, with affrright,
> The shrieks of death thro' BERKELEY's ROOFS that ring,
> Shrieks of an agonizing king! "

The deposed Edward was brought here on the 5th of April, 1327. It is said that Lord Berkeley was ordered to hold no intercourse with him, and to deliver up the care of the castle to Maltravers and Gurnay, keepers of the degraded monarch. These orders, we are told, he obeyed, and retired for a time to some private residence, at no great distance. The king was confined to a small room, still remaining in the castle, and in that room he died, as is believed, in consequence of the most atrocious violence committed by Maltravers and Gurnay. His death is thought to have taken

The Hall, Berkeley Castle

place on the 21st of September, 1327, but it was kept secret for some time, and the whole of the circumstances attending his dissolutions are involved in great obscurity. After his decease his heart was enclosed in a silver vessel, and the Berkeley family formed part of the procession which attended the royal corpse to the place of its interment, in the abbey-church of Gloucester.

Although Lord Berkeley was formally acquitted of any active participation in the measures which caused the death of the king, it is observable that he entertained at this castle Queen Isabel and Mortimer her paramour, shortly after the decease of Edward! Few persons will envy this nobleman the circumstances of grandeur with which he was enabled to entertain visiters so callous to all the common feelings of humanity, but, in relation to the appearance of the castle at that time, it may be observed that he kept twelve knights to wait upon his person, each of whom was attended by two servants and a page. He had twenty-four esquires, each having an under-servant and horse. The entire family consisted of about three hundred persons, besides husbandmen, who also dieted at his board. It is recorded, by Sir R. Atkyns, that this lord was very "active at all commissions of justice!" He was, likewise, greatly praised by ecclesiastics, for his benefactions to the church.

In the fifth year of King Henry V. a law-suit was commenced, between Lord Berkeley and a female cousin, the heiress of the family, which was continued by the posterity of the opposed parties, and lasted 192 years! During these ages of legal contest, the plaintiff's party, as a solace for the tardiness of the courts, several times laid siege to the castle.

Margaret, Queen of Henry VI. stopped here for a short time, when on her way from Bristol to the disastrous field of Tewkesbury. Henry VII. visited this place, as did also Queen Elizabeth, in the fifteenth year of her reign. Lord Berkeley, for the queen's entertainment, "had a stately game of red deer" in the park adjoining.

In the civil wars of the seventeenth century the castle was garrisoned on the side of the king, and held in control all this part of the county. It underwent a siege from Colonel Massie, one of the most able officers in the Commonwealth army, and is said to have surrendered to Sir Charles Lucas, on the 25th of September 1645, after a defence of nine days.

The following notice of a fire which occurred, about half a century since, is extracted from a letter of Horace Walpole to Mr. Cole, dated 1774. "The castle is much smaller, than I expected, but very entire, except a small part burned two years ago, while the present earl was in the house. The fire began in the housekeeper's room, who never appeared more; but as she was strict over the servants, and not a bone of her was found, it was supposed that she was murdered, and the body conveyed away."

The Castle of Berkeley is a large but irregular pile, consisting chiefly of a keep, and ranges of various embattled buildings, with two baileys, or courts. The entrance is conducted through a gate-house, strongly machicolated, and connected with the keep.

The keep approaches in form to that of the Roman D, and has four towers, three of which are semicircular and one square. That on the north was rebuilt in the reign of Edward III. and has been termed Thorpe's tower, because, as is said, the Thorpes of *Wanswell*, in this county and neighbourhood, held their manor by the tenure of guarding this part of the castle. The great stair-case is composed of stone, and formed in the square tower. On the right hand of this staircase is the room in which it is said Edward II. met his fate. This is a small and gloomy apartment, thus noticed by Lord Orford, in the letter cited above. "It is a dismal chamber, almost at the top of the house, quite detached, and to be approached only by a kind of foot-bridge, and from that descends a large flight of steps, that terminate on strong gates; exactly a situation for a *corps de garde*. In that room they shew you a cast of a face in plaister, and tell you it was taken from Edward's. I was not quite so easy of faith about that: for it is evidently a face of Charles the First's." This cast is still shown, and several succeeding writers have copied Lord Orford's opinion, as to the face for which it was designed; but we believe that the cast was, in reality, taken from the effigies of Edward, on his tomb in Gloucester cathedral.

The keep is not insulated, as in many early Norman castles, but stands upon the outward wall of the area: a mode of disposal often seen in castellated structures designed in the twelfth century. It is observed by Mr. Fosbroke that the Roman method of filling the inner part, or medium, of the walls with fluid mortar, occurs here.

The principal court, or area, is very irregular in outline, and is, we are informed, about 140 yards round. The chief ornament of this court is the venerable front of the hall, which, together with contiguous parts of the structure, is represented in one of our engraved views. Our second engraving displays the interior of this noble baronial hall; and the examiner will perceive that much of the antient character is still preserved. It is 48 feet in length, and 33 in width, and was erected about the eighteenth of Edward III. by Thomas, Lord Berkeley. Adjoining is the chapel of St. Mary, of smaller dimensions than the place of family banquet and recreation; it being no more than 36 feet in length, and 24 in width.

It must be observed that there was, also, a more antient chapel, situated in the keep, which is now used as the evidence room.

The apartments of the castle are very numerous, but, chiefly with the exception of the hall, are of confined proportions and a gloomy character. In different parts are many portraits of the Berkeley family; and some of the furniture is curious from its antiquity. Several old and magnificent bedsteads are among the principal articles shewn to visiters. One of these bears the date of 1530, and is richly adorned and gilt.

The Barony of Berkeley descends, with the lands, to the heirs male only. The castle is the residence of Colonel William Fitzhardinge Berkeley.

33

Cleve Hill

THE SEAT OF DANIEL CAVE ESQ. M.A.

CLEVE HILL is distant from Bristol about four miles, towards the north-east, and is one of the finest seats in the immediate vicinity of that city. The house is situated in the parish of Mangotsfield, and near the turnpike-road leading to Chipping-Sodbury.

The domain of Cleve Hill was purchased in the reign of James I. by William Player, Esq. from the family of Blount, long seated in the neighbouring parish of Bitton. By his descendant, it was sold to Charles Bragge, Esq. father of the Right Hon. Charles Bragge Bathurst, M.P. &c. of Lydney Park, in this county, and was subsequently transferred by purchase, together with the adjoining property of Cleve Dale, to Stephen Cave, Esq. who has since relinquished it in favour of his son, the present proprietor.

A view of the mansion, as it appeared at the commencement of the eighteenth century, is given in the History of Gloucestershire, by Sir Robert Atkyns. It was then the seat of William Player, Esq. but the building, though apparently spacious, had little pretensions to beauty. The plantations, consisting of long avenues and formal rows of trees, were very extensive; and here we curiously see, in an early stage of growth, those components of sylvan beauty which, now that the right lines are broken, form the pride of the domain. A large court, in front of the house, was inclosed by high walls; and a wide paved footway led from the great outward gate to the principal door of entrance. A footway of this description is a frequent feature in mansions erected in the last half of the seventeenth century; and so tedious a length of approach, in full view of the hall of reception, was evidently designed for a kind of state purpose. Here the visitors, treading the parade in measured steps, had full room and opportunity for a display of those gorgeous brocades, and other boldly figured and highly coloured articles of attire, which appeared to be intended for an open place of exhibition, and were certainly calculated for distant effect.

All traces of cold formality, and laboured vanity of display, have now given place to the true elegance of natural simplicity, and the genius of classic refinement. Since the date of Sir Robert's engraving, the mansion has been re-edified, with the exception of some of the secondary bed-rooms and the offices. The two fronts shewn in the annexed view were erected about the year 1717, and are of proportions eminently fine. The architectural enrichments are Grecian, and each elevation presents an admirable example in that style of design.

This residence, although of considerable magnitude, is arranged, on the interior, with a view to family comfort, rather than to the ostentation of magnificence. It is trite to remark, that domestic architecture is assistant in developing the history of national manners, but we cannot refrain from observing, that an arrangement like that which we have described as prevailing at this place, presents an agreeable memorial of the habits of English gentility, in the early part of the eighteenth century. For a studied air of comfort, in the disposal of a house on so large a scale, it would be almost vain to look beyond our own island; and it is with an honest emotion of

CLEVE HILL

patriotic pride we find, that this peculiar characteristic of the English mansion is, in the present, and many other instances, attained without any perceptible sacrifice of true dignity.

The good taste of a recent period has added greatly to the attractions and comforts of this elegant abode. The library comprises several thousand volumes, in the best editions of the classics, and of the most esteemed authors, in Italian, French and English literature. There are, also, a few pictures by good masters; and several of the apartments are adorned with sculpture, collected by Mr. Cave, in Italy.

The gardens and pleasure-grounds consist of about ten acres, and are laid out with a correctness of judgment that cannot be duly appreciated, without a comparison of their present mode of disposal with that exhibited in the view preserved by Sir R. Atkyns. Many of the trees, which wrap parts of this domain in a soothing shade, are now of dimensions unusually large, and are still of a flourishing growth. The hot-houses and conservatories are on an extensive scale; and there is, likewise, a spacious aviary. The richly-wooded lands contiguous to this seat, are bounded by the Frome, here a stream of a retiring character, productive of much picturesque beauty.

The hamlet of Downend, in this parish, has long been celebrated for its quarries of close-grained sand-stone used for paving, and also for gate-pillars and similar purposes. Good specimens of the stone are seen in the columns of an entrance-lodge at Cleve Hill, which are composed of single blocks.

At Bury Hill, also in the parish of Mangotsfield, is a small Roman Camp, attributed to Ostorius.

BOXWELL COURT

34

Boxwell Court

THE SEAT OF THE REV. RICHARD HUNTLEY, M.A.

THE parish of Boxwell lies between Tetbury and Wotton-under-edge, at the distance of about four miles from the last-named town. The village occupies a station most attractively rural and picturesque, at the head of a tranquil vale, fertilized by a rill of devious progress, and sheltered by surrounding hills and tracts of woodland.

The name is written Boxewelle, in Domesday, and is thought to be derived from the natural circumstance of a copious spring, issuing from a wood of box-trees. This wood contains, by estimation, about twenty acres. It is still flourishing, and is, perhaps, the most extensive wood of its kind in England, now that the number of trees at Boxhill, in Surrey, has suffered by recent encroachments. The spring that issues from this wood speedily receives the contribution of a rivulet from Lasborough, and, after uniting its waters with a stream which proceeds from Kilcot, becomes sufficiently important to receive a name, and falls into the Severn, near Berkeley, under the designation of the Berkeley Avon. It was formerly, throughout its course, well known to be prolific of trout, but, since the erection of many clothing mills on its banks, that delicate fish is to be found only in the higher parts of the water, which have, hitherto, escaped the influence of the contaminating ingredients used in the clothing munufacture.

At the date of the great national record termed Domesday, this parish and manor appertained to the abbey of Gloucester, and the abbot subsequently procured here the privilege of free-warren. Previously, however, to the dissolution of monastic houses, the manor belonged, partly in fee, and partly under a lease from the abbey, to John Huntley, styled de la Rea, whose son and heir, also named John, in the thirty-fourth of Henry VIII. demised this property for 92 years to Henry, his younger son. The moiety in lease was granted by Queen Elizabeth, to persons named Bennet and Swaine, who sold it to Sir Walter Raleigh. Upon the attainder of that celebrated man, it was regranted to Vanlore and Blake, by the former of whom it was conveyed, in the tenth of James I. to George Huntley; and since that period, the manor, together with the advowson of the rectory, has descended in the Huntley family.

This respectable family derive their descent from the Huntleys of Haddock, in Monmouthshire; and were also, as we are informed by Mr. Fosbroke, lords of the manor of Huntley, in this county, previous to the date of the existing Tower records. John Huntley, designated de la Rea, ancestor of the Gloucestershire branches, was seated at *the Rye*, near Gloucester; and his son (the father of Henry Huntley, Esq. the first of this family that settled at Boxwell) was of Standish, in this county, of which manor he was tenant under the abbey of Gloucester. The Rev. Richard Huntley, M.A. the present proprietor, and also rector of Boxwell and of Dodington, is tenth lord of this manor, in lineal succession from John Huntley de la Rea. His arms are shewn at the bottom of the annexed engraving, quartering Langley of Siddington, and Ferrers of Groby.

The manor-house, of which building we present a view, is finely situated on an eminence, among swelling hills of various graceful forms, all of which adorn its prospects, whilst some afford it a partial shelter. This structure was chiefly erected by John Huntley de la Rea, in the fifteenth century, and preserved its antient character until the year 1796, at which time we regret to say that the exterior was modernized.

Some traces of antiquity, though not of an age so remote as that of the founder, are still to be seen within several of the apartments. The chimney-piece of the dining room, presents the most curious of these vestiges. It is carved in free stone, and is of the time of Elizabeth. On each side of the fire-place rise, from pedestals ornamented with various devices in the style often called gothic, two pillars of the Ionic order, supporting an entablature, charged with the double rose of England, and other heraldic bearings. This entablature on each side becomes, in turn, the basement of two Caryatides, which support another entablature, decorated, also, with heraldic embellishments, and approaching the ceiling. In the centre, between two plainer shields, appear the family coat, helmet and crest, in the midst of foliage carved with admirable boldness and relief.

The dining-room likewise contains the following pictures, well entitled to notice:

> A spirited portrait of *Bishop Warburton*, whom this family represents; and a portrait of his son, by Sir Joshua Reynolds.
>
> An excellent portrait of *Edward Chandler, Bishop of Durham*, from whom Mr. Huntley is maternally descended.
>
> Over the side-board is a very fine painting, supposed by Weeninx, the subject *a black servant, carrying fruit.*
>
> In another room is a good portrait of *Elizabeth Chandler*, wife of Matthew Huntley, Esq. by Sir Godfrey Kneller.

It is traditionally said by Leland that a nunnery existed here before the Conquest, which was destroyed by the Danes. Some marked inequalities in the surface of a meadow, have been supposed to denote the site of that religious house. On digging very recently in that quarter, in consequence of some alterations that have been there effected, the skeleton of a female was found, enclosed in a well-wrought stone coffin.

In the adjoining hamlet of LEIGHTERTON a large barrow was opened, about the year 1690, by Matthew Huntley, Esq. and was found to contain three arched vaults, each being the receptacle of an urn, in which were ashes, and bones that had undergone cremation.

It may not be superfluous to observe that the *Brambling,* a bird rarely seen in the southern parts of Britain, migrates hither in the winter, for the shelter of the Box-wood.

35

Alderley House

THE SEAT OF ROBERT HALE BLAGDON HALE, ESQ.

THE parish of Alderley, entitled to no ordinary a degree of veneration, as the birth-place, and favourite residence, of the wise, upright and benevolent Sir Matthew Hale, is situated in the southern part of this county, at the distance of two miles from the town of Wotton-under-edge. The parish is finely various in surface, abounding in alternations of hill and dale; and has for its limits, on the north and south, two small brooks, which, uniting their streams to the west of the village, fall into the Severn near Berkeley, being known, after their junction, by the common name of the Avon.

The manor, at the time of the Norman Survey, formed part of the large possessions of Milo Crispin. It afterwards belonged to the family of de Chansey, through several descents; from whom it passed to the Stanshawes. The first of this family, mentioned in connexion with Alderley, is Robert Stanshawe, who died in the twelfth of Edward IV. Joan, his widow, with a second husband, named Robert Bodisaunt, passed the manor, by fine, in the fourteenth of Henry VII. to Richard Becket and others, who again alienated to —— Pointz. The family of Pointz held it for several generations. Of this family (likewise noticed in our account of Newark Park) was Robert Pointz, a zealous Romanist, and author of several religious books. He was born at Alderley, and became perpetual Fellow of New College, in 1554; but afterwards settled at Lovain, in Brabant.

Robert, son of Sir Nicholas Pointz, sold this estate to Matthew Rogers; whose brother and heir again sold it to —— Barker, Esq. of Fairford. Mr. Barker conveyed it to Sir Matthew Hale, in exchange for the manor of Meysey Hampton; and it has ever since remained in the family of that distinguished person. Matthew Hale, Esq. dying in 1784, left the property to John Blagdon Hale, Esq. who had married his niece and heiress and who assumed, by royal licence, the arms and surname of Hale.

Alderley House, of which we present a view, was erected about the year 1779, by the late Matthew Hale, Esq. This is a spacious and respectable structure, having few ornaments on the exterior, but where decoration is used the Grecian style has been adopted. It is now in the occupation of the Rev. James Phelps, and does not contain any portraits of the Hale family, except a whole length, by Gainsborough, of Matthew Hale, Esq. who died here in the year 1784. The grounds and plantations comprise about fifteen acres, and are disposed with great accuracy of judgment and delicacy of taste.

An engraved view of the antient mansion of Alderley, in which Sir Matthew Hale passed the serene days of his leisure from public duties, is given in the history of this county by Sir R. Atkyns. The seat, when a view was taken for that work, was the residence of Mrs. Hale, widow to the grandson of the lord chief justice. The print exhibits the garden-front of a spacious. building, having numerous large-casements, and many attic windows, projecting from the roof.

ALDERLEY HOUSE

The gardens have several ascending terraces, and are designed with great formality, the parterres being nicely proportioned by line and rule, and each tree having its fellow, as if the whole had been planted in pairs. On the borders of the domain are long avenues, the trees of which appear to be of early growth.

That mansion is still standing, and is situated near the church. It is at present occupied by the brother of Mr. R. H. Blagdon Hale; and, until about two years back, the building remained in the same state as when inhabited by the lord chief justice. It has now undergone considerable alterations, the whole of which may be improvements, but still many examiners will be induced to regret that they can no longer behold this interesting structure, in all the antient and venerable simplicity of its character. It is obvious that even deformity becomes sanctified by an association with the memorable talent, or moral worth, of a long-past age. Thus, we should be induced to prefer to all the graces of modern gardening, the walks, however formal, which afforded places of exercise and recreation to the great and good Sir Matthew Hale, when meditating on the transactions of days devoted to his God and his country.

The biography of this eminent native of Alderley, is so well known, through the labours of Burnet, Runnington, and minor writers, that it cannot be necessary for us to enter on particulars, in this place, but some few remarks are unavoidable. Sir Matthew Hale, Knight, lord chief baron and lord chief justice, was son of Robert Hale, Esq. and Joan, daughter of Matthew Pointz, Esq. of Alderley. Concerning his ancestry, it is said by Sir R Atkyns, that "the family of the Hales has been of antient standing in this county, and always esteemed for their probity and charity." He received the early part of his education at the neighbouring town of Wotton-under-edge, and was afterwards of Magdalen Hall. We have already observed that he had the pleasure of regaining, for himself and his descendants, the manorial property which had belonged to the family of his mother. The beneficence with which, in his retirement at Alderley, he enjoyed the advantages of an honourable prosperity, has been celebrated by writers whose works are likely to prove lasting, if only from the merit of their subject. The high renown of his public worth and private virtues, among his contemporaries, may be illustrated by an anecdote, connected with this place.—It is recorded that a clergyman, 80 years of age, "walked all the way from Yorkshire, *to see the residence of the lord chief justice.*" It is observed by Sir R. Atkyns, who was, in every point of view, a competent judge of his merits, "that if Gloucestershire has not yielded so many eminent men as some other counties, yet this great person may go for many: *Quantum instar in illo est!*"

Sir Matthew Hale died in 1676, and was buried in the church-yard of Alderley, that place of sepulture having been chosen by himself. Over his remains was erected a monument of black and white marble, bearing this unostentatious inscription:

Hic inhumatur corpus Mathœi Hale, Militis,
(Roberti Hale, et Johannæ uxoris ejus, filii unici)
nati in hâc parochia de Alderly 1° Nov. 1609, denati
vero ibidem 25, Dec. 1676, Ætat. suæ 67.

HIGH STREET, BRISTOL

36

Bristol

THIS great commercial City is erected upon ground formerly constituting parts of the counties of Gloucester and Somerset, but was created a distinct county of itself by King Edward III. in the year 1373. As regards levies of the militia, however, it is still included in Gloucestershire. It is seated upon the confluence of the rivers Avon and Froom, which, at the distance of about ten miles from the bridge of this city, discharge their waters into the estuary termed the Bristol Channel.

Bristol claims a British origin, but does not appear to have been adopted by the Romans, who had a station in its vicinity. Under the domination of the Anglo-Saxons it arose to some distinction, and constituted a frontier town, and the principal sea-port, of the extensive kingdom of Wessex. When a frequent communication was opened between Britain and Ireland, in the seventh century, this port acquired a fresh source of prosperity, as the chief resort of vessels sailing between the two countries. From this circumstance Bristol enumerates, amongst its various honours, the occasional sojourn within its walls of several sovereigns, and other eminent personages, in the early and middle ages of our national history. Many particulars, connected with those eras in its annals, are noticed by the present writer in the topographical work entitled the "Beauties of Ireland."

A castle existed here before the conquest, which, on the entry of the Normans, was held by Brictric, to whose injurious treatment, at the instigation of Maud, queen of William I. we have adverted in our account of Thornbury Castle. His estates, including this castle, were settled on that queen by her triumphant consort. In Domesday-book the citizens are termed burgesses, and we are there told that "Bristow, with Barton, paid to the King 100 marks of silver."

In the wars between Stephen and the Empress Maud, the inhabitants of Bristol declared against the existing government; and it appears that the castle experienced a siege from the King in person, but was possessed, through the most important parts of those contests, by the Empress, for whom it constituted a strong and useful hold.

Henry II. granted to the burgesses a charter, exempting them and their goods from the payment of toll, passage, and custom, throughout his whole land of England, Normandy, and Wales. It is said, by William of Malmsbury, that Bristol was at this time full of ships from Ireland, Norway, and other parts of Europe, which brought hither great commerce and much foreign wealth. Edward I. after his memorable reduction of the Welsh, in 1283, repaired to this place, and here celebrated the festivities of Christmas, and held a parliament. In 1362, an event occurred, of more solid import to the city than the visits of princes. In that year the staple of wool was established here by King Edward III. The mayor, on this occasion, received the additional title of "Mayor of the Staple of Bristol," with the privilege of holding a court, called the Staple Court. It is ascertained that, in the fifteenth century, the merchants were concerned largely in a trade with Spain, to which country they exported cloths, called Bristol drapery. In 1581, manufactories of pins and stockings were established here.

That the active artificers of Bristol had been long engaged in ship-building is unquestionable, and they attained particular celebrity in the seventeenth century. It is recorded that, in various periods of that century, ships of war were launched at this port.—We regret to interrupt remarks on the happy procedure of manufactures and commercial prosperity with tales of commotion and bloodshed, but the task of the topographer, like the web of life, is composed of a "mingled yarn," and he must patiently trace the works effected by varying passions, evil as well as good.— In 1642, the castle and walls were repaired by the magistrates, with the ostensible intent of securing the place for King Charles I. who, in that year, set up the royal standard; but it was soon discovered that the majority of the inhabitants, disgusted with the assumptions of the court, were desirous of taking side with the opposite party. We have, in our account of Gloucester, had occasion to remark the activity of the females of this part of England, in the wars of the seventeenth century. The ladies of Bristol participated in the spirit of their neighbours. Whilst the city yet hesitated in its choice of party, Mrs. Mayoress, and many of her lady-friends, entered the Tolsey, where the magistrates were assembled in council, and petitioned that the parliament's army might be received within the walls! It was received accordingly; and in July of the following year, the city was besieged by an army, 20,000 strong, under Prince Rupert and the Marquis of Hertford. The defence was very gallantly conducted for three days; but, on the fourth, the place was unexpectedly surrendered, through either the treachery or cowardice of Col. Fiennes, the governor, who was put to trial for this offence, and condemned to die, but was finally suffered to retire beyond the seas.

In 1645, took place the second siege of Bristol. The city was assailed by Fairfax and Cromwell, and was defended by Prince Rupert. This formed a memorable era in the lamented civil war between the court and the people. The King's affairs had lately received a severe shock from his defeat at Naseby, and nearly his last hope depended on the successful resistance of this important city. The besiegers stormed the outworks with great fury, but with only partial success; and the city was still firm, and maintained by an undaunted garrison, when, to the surprise of all parties, Prince Rupert desired a parley, and surrendered by treaty. Thus, in the last, as well as in the first, great military transaction of the civil war, the incapacity of this prince proved of serious injury to his royal relative. With such a queen as Henrietta for his counsel, and such a nephew as Prince Rupert for a confidential commander, the King's affairs naturally fell to utter ruin.

Bristol, from its situation on the banks of the Avon, may be described as occupying ground relatively low; but no inconvenience occurs from this circumstance; as the tract on which it stands undulates into several hills, favourable to the beauty of the city and the health of its inhabitants. The old town, now forming merely the *nucleus* of this great and populous city, was ineligibly designed and constructed in most respects, perhaps even without the exception of commercial uses. Nor are the large additions, which have been progressively made, uniformly gratifying to the critical examiner; but many of the modern squares, streets, and buildings are unquestionably ornamental; and Bristol, in its present state, may, on the whole, be said to possess the architectural characteristics required from its rank and station, as a commercial city of the first class.

Its boundaries, constituting its own peculiar county, extend to a circumference of about seven miles, exclusive of its jurisdiction by water, which reaches as far as the two islands named respectively Flat and Steep Holm. Within the city-boundaries are seventeen parishes, to which, in the consideration of the casual spectator, must be added, as apparent parts of Bristol, the outparishes of St. James, and St. Philip-and-James, together with the adjacent parishes of Bedminster and Clifton. Bristol, in this point of view, contains ten squares, and about seven hundred and twenty streets, lanes, courts, and *places,* possessing individual appellations. The public structures are highly respectable in character; and two of the Churches (namely, the Cathedral and St. Mary Redcliff) are admirable specimens of antient architecture. The churches are nineteen in number, besides the suburban churches and chapels of Bedminster, Clifton, Dowry-square, and the Orphan Asylum. There are, also, thirty dissenting meeting-houses, and a chapel for French protestants, in which is adopted the liturgy of the church of England.

In the VIEWS we present we have selected subjects calculated to convey ideas respecting the general character of this busy city, rather than such as merely display individual buildings, however beautiful those separate objects may be justly considered.

The history of the CATHEDRAL is connected with that of an *Augustinian monastery,* founded in 1140, by Robert Fitzharding, first Lord Berkeley. The original buildings were completed in six years from the date of the foundation. The site of this monastery, together with the extent and appropriation of its remains, independent of the church, are thus noticed by Mr. Barrett, in his essay towards a History of Bristol. "It was built on a rising ground, with a delightful prospect of the hills around, in the north-west suburb of the city. The area of the buildings, appropriated for the abbot and his monks, was very large and extensive; as by the rule of St. Augustin, to whom it was dedicated, they were to live here together in common. The walls, and part of the large refectory, or dining room, now converted into a prebendal house; the abbot's house, now partly rebuilt and made a palace for the bishop's residence; two sides of the cloister, with a curious chapter-house, and some beautiful arches and gateways; are still to be seen."

The monastery thus founded by Fitzharding, was enriched with the grants of various estates from succeeding lords of Berkeley, nearly down to the period of the Reformation; and was, likewise, favoured with valuable donations from Kings Henry and John, and other distinguished personages. It was dissolved in 1539.

Three years after the date at which the monastery was suppressed, King Henry VIII. erected Bristol into an episcopal see; and, from the time of such an erection only, is this place strictly entitled to the appellation of a city. The church of the former monastic house was established as the cathedral of the new diocess. The building, in its present state, consists of a choir, its aisles, and a transept, surmounted by a fine, but not lofty, tower. The whole of the structure to the west of the tower was taken down, at some period not precisely ascertained, but tradition and probability equally point to the years intervening between the suppression of monasteries and the foundation of this see.

Chiefly with the exception of some parts of the chapter-house, and arches and pillars near the entrance of that room, the buildings of the cathedral are in the pointed style. Where affluent resources were at command, it was by no means unusual for a monastic brotherhood to re-edify its church, in this new and graceful mode of architecture, although the existing pile was sufficiently capacious in its dimensions, and quite uninjured by time. Thus, the rebuilding of this church was commenced in 1311, the second year in the reign of Edward II. and about one hundred and sixty-three years after its first erection. The author of a very amusing and useful work, recently published, under the title of "A Chronological Outline of the History of Bristol," is of opinion that past inquirers have been mistaken in estimating the age of this structure, and that, in reality, little more was effected in the early part of the fourteenth century than the addition of "some abutments and their pinnacles ;" but his arguments are not satisfactory to the architectural antiquary.

BRISTOL

The effect of the interior is much deteriorated by the loss of the western part, but is still not destitute of beauty and solemn grandeur. The windows are adorned with much rich tracery; and it has been remarked, as a feature peculiar to this cathedral, that the ceilings of the choir, aisles, and transept are of uniform height. If the altitude of those parts of the building were greater, the display proceeding from this uniformity could scarcely fail to surprise and delight the spectator, in a very unusual degree. The east window is adorned with painted glass, as are, likewise, several windows in the north and south aisles. The subjects are chiefly representations of passages in the Old and New Testaments. It is said that the glass for one of these windows was presented to the church by Eleanor Gwyn, the protestant mistress of Charles II. The stalls in the choir, thirty-four in number, were erected in 1542.—The entrance to the chapter-house, which we have noticed as one of the few remaining parts of the original structure, has semi-circular arches, sustained by clustered pillars. The *Elder Lady Chapel*, on the north side of the cathedral, is likewise supposed to have constituted part of Fitzharding's building.

There are some monuments of considerable interest, and numerous mural tablets. Amongst the persons here buried are many of the Lords Berkeley, and several abbots of the dissolved monastery. Few monuments of a modern date in this cathedral attract so much notice as that to "*Mrs. Elizabeth Draper*, in whom Genius and Benevolence were united. She died August 3rd, 1778, aged thirty-five." The monument was executed by Bacon. Two female figures, in alto relievo, stand on the sides of a pedestal, that supports an urn adorned with wreathed flowers. On the right is a figure, representing Genius; and on the left is the statue of Benevolence, contemplating a nest, in which the pelican feeds its young with blood from its own breast.—The lady thus commemorated was wife of Daniel Draper, Esq. a barrister at Bombay, and will long be recollected, by the admirers of romantic sentiment expressed in elegant language, as the *Eliza* of Sterne.—In the north aisle is a monument to *Mrs. Mason*, wife of the Rev. William Mason, author of Caractacus and other poems, with a pleasing inscription, in verse, from the pen of her husband.—The choir is chiefly occupied by the remains of the bishops of this diocese.

The Church of *St. Mary Redcliff*, originally a chapel to Bedminster, is justly esteemed as one of the finest parochial churches in the kingdom. This beautiful example of pointed architecture, when that mode of building had attained its highest stage of perfection (plenitude without redundancy of decoration) was progressively erected in the fourteenth century, chiefly under the auspices of the Mayors, and other civic officers of Bristol; and it should ever be viewed as the proudest trophy, possessed by any commercial town, of the zealous piety, and princely munificence, with which the merchants of a past age devoted to public and religious uses a portion of the wealth derived from a local exercise of industrious habits. To this splendid and costly pile the family of Canynges were principal contributors.

It is built in the form of a cross, and has a lady-chapel at the eastern end. The exquisite lightness and symmetry of this edifice, and the delicacy and judicious disposal of its abundant enrichments, cannot fail to gratify the examiner, in precisely the same ratio as he may excel in taste, judgment, and architectural information. Could Sir Christopher Wren have seen this triumph of art, and still have termed the pointed mode of design a *barbarous* style of architecture?

Our limits prevent us from entering on any resemblance of a descriptive analysis of the various features, which, in this charming structure, combine towards the production of a transcendant general effect; but we collect some few particulars of miscellaneous intelligence, chiefly relating to its history. In Ricart's Kalendar of the Mayors it is said, that, in 1736, "William Canynges builded the body of Redcliff Church, from the cross-iles downwarde; and so the church was finished as it is nowe;" meaning the 18th of Edward IV. The original height of the steeple was two hundred and fifty feet; but during a storm which visited Bristol in 1446, the upper part of the spire was blown down; and this mutilation has been suffered to remain unremedied, to the regret of every spectator.—Over the north porch is the Muniment-room, an unglazed apartment, in which Chatterton professed to have found the poems, given to the world as the productions of Thomas Rowley, a monk of the fifteenth century. In the "Chronological Outline" it is said that, in the year 1727, "a notion prevailed that title-deeds, &c. were enclosed in Mr. Canynge's cofre, deposited, with other chests, in the Muniment-room. Such deeds as appeared of value were removed to the vestry-room. The uncle of Chatterton's father was then sexton of the church." We shall again slightly notice this subject, when speaking of Chatterton as a native of Bristol.

There were, in this church, altars respectively dedicated to St. Stephen; St. Catherine; St. Blaze; St. Nicholas; and St. George. Among the principal persons buried within these walls, and commemorated by monuments, must be mentioned several of the family of Canynges, and *Sir William Penn*, father of W. Penn, founder of Pennsylvania. He died Sept. 16, 1670, in the 50th year of his age.—Over the altar are paintings by Hogarth and Tresham. Those by Hogarth represent Christ and the Woman of Samaria; the Sealing of the Tomb; and the Resurrection. They were placed in the church in 1756, at which time Hogarth received for painting them 500 guineas. That by Tresham represents Christ raising the daughter of Jairus, and was presented to this church by Sir Clifton Wintringham, Bart.

The Public Buildings, for the administration of Justice, and for Commercial uses, are numerous, and suited to the real importance of the city in which they are placed. The *Guildhall* is a spacious structure, of considerable antiquity. The first mention of such a building in Bristol occurs in 1313. This Hall was newly fronted in 1813, at which time was taken down a front that had been erected preparatory to a visit of Queen Elizabeth, in 1574. The *Council-house* is a handsome and appropriate edifice, commenced in 1824, after the designs of Robert Smirke, architect. In the Chamber are about thirty portraits of royal and noble persons, together with those of several magistrates and distinguished inhabitants of Bristol. The most antient is that of Thomas White, Mayor in 1529. Perhaps the most interesting is that of the benevolent EDWARD COLSTON, Esq. whose extensive charities are an honour, not only to this city, but to the name of BRITISH MERCHANT. Notwithstanding his princely bounties, Mr. Colston left more than £100,000 among his relations. He died in 1721, at the age of eighty-five. The *Custom-house* is a substantial and capacious building, having a principal room, about seventy feet in length. The *Exchange* was commenced in 1740, and completed 1743, after the designs of Mr. Wood, of Bath. The cost was nearly £50,000. This is a spacious and highly-ornamented structure. The place for the assembly of merchants is within an extensive range of columns, of the Corinthian order, which form a peristyle, capable of containing about fourteen hundred persons. The *Merchants' Hall* is a handsome building of freestone, erected in 1701, but considerably improved in recent years. In the outer hall is a portrait of the late Edward Colston. The *Commercial-rooms*, opened in 1811, were built after, the designs of Mr. C. A. Busby.

The Charitable Foundations, and Schools for Gratuitous Education, are very numerous, and are equally honourable to those who have successfully cultivated the advantages of this mercantile city, and beneficial to various classes of the suffering and indigent.

The *City Library*, in King Street, was founded in 1613, by an individual, named Robert Redwood; but the "Bristol Library-Society" was not formed until 1772. Many gifts of books have been made at different periods, and the building was augmented in 1786. The *Bristol Philosophical and Literary Institution* was established in 1820. A handsome building, for the use of this society, was completed in 1822, under the direction of Mr. Charles Robert Cockerell, architect.

The principal *bridge* is a handsome stone building, consisting of three arches, the central of which is an elliptic of fifty feet span. It was completed, in its present form, in 1768.

The *Theatre Royal*, situated in King Street, was opened in 1766, on which occasion a prologue and epilogue were written by Garrick. More than 5000*l.* were expended in the erection of this well-designed and handsome playhouse. In 1777 an act was passed, to enable his Majesty to licence a theatre in this city.

Bristol is adorned with statues of Kings William III. and George III. The statue of William is situated in Queen's Square, and that of the late King in Portland Square.

The trading facilities of this city were greatly advanced by an act of parliament, passed in 1803, for converting the rivers Avon and Froom, into a Floating-harbour, by cutting a new course for the Avon, from the line of the city-boundary eastward, to the Red Clift westward. The works were begun in 1804, and finished in 1809. This floating harbour is two miles and a half in length, and ranks amongst the most important works of the kind in Europe.

Bristol first arose to consequence as a commercial port; and, from the activity and spirit of enterprize which have characterized its mercantile inhabitants, it progressively attained a station in the list of trading cities, second only to that of the metropolis. It is evident that commercial prosperity must fluctuate with many circumstances of national advance or retrocession; and it is equally obvious that, as a country increases in population and wealth, new marts will arise, and the stream of commerce become too large to flow, as in more antient and simple times, through one channel. Thus, the trade of Bristol has not failed to experience some vicissitudes; and in Liverpool this city has found a rival, equally powerful in energies and opportunities. Still, in despite of occasional clouds, and notwithstanding the successful efforts of its competitor, this port remains, as in the antient days of its uncontested celebrity, renowned for extent of foreign commerce and home trade. Its foreign connexions are chiefly with the West Indies, North America, Hamburgh, and the Baltic. With Ireland it has a large commercial intercourse. It chiefly supplies South Wales with articles of importation, and is the emporium of traffic in the West of England.

The ship-builders of this port have continued to maintain a high reputation, and numerous men-of-war were launched here in the last century. Sugar-houses; brass and iron founderies; distilleries; glass-houses; and various manufactories, are conducted on a large scale.

Bristol has recently obtained a considerable improvement, from the adoption of gas, in lighting the streets. It is internally governed by a Mayor; two Sheriffs; twelve Aldermen; and a certain number of Common Council; forming, in the whole, a body corporate of forty-three persons. It has, also, the honour of a Lord High Steward, which dignified office is at present filled by Lord Grenville. Several charters have been granted to the citizens, the last of which was obtained from Queen Anne, in 1710. The privileged burgesses send two members to parliament; and attain their privileges by the possession of a freehold by parentage, as sons of freemen; by serving an apprenticeship to a freeman; or by marrying a freeman's daughter. The total number of inhabitants (independent of the suburban parishes) as returned in the year 1821, was 52,889. The total number in the suburban parishes, including Clifton, was, in the same year, 33,154. Bristol gives the title of Marquess and Earl to the family of Hervey.

It has been said that "the number of great men, in every department of human knowledge, which Bristol has produced, probably exceeds that of any other place of equal extent in this kingdom, perhaps in the civilized world." We enumerate a few of these distinguished natives, as the best tribute of respect to a city which, assuredly, furnishes in an unusual degree for a place devoted to commerce, subjects of pleasing intellectual associations.

Sebastian Cabot, the real discoverer of North America, born in 1477.

William of Worcester, sometimes called, from his maternal descent, William Botoner, who flourished in the fifteenth century.

William Grocyne, the friend of Erasmus, and the first public professor of Greek in the University of Oxford. Born about 1440.

The philanthropist, *Edward Colston,* who expended 140,000*l.* in acts of benevolence. Born in 1636.

Thomas Chatterton, born in 1752. So much has been written upon the subject of Chatterton and his publications, that we should refrain from extended remarks, even if our limits allowed of such an indulgence. A trifling, but novel and not uninteresting particular, is afforded by Mr. Evans, in his *Chronological Outline.* "It has not before found a place in print that Chatterton's favourite book-shop was that of Mr. Goodall, in Tower-lane. Here (as Mr. Goodall informed the writer) our youthful poet passed many hours in a day, buying such books as came within his means, and sitting to read those which he either did not wish to possess, or could not afford to purchase. He was particularly attached to one book, on Saxon manners and customs." We presume it is universally admitted that the works published by Chatterton, under the names of Rowley and other supposed antient writers, were not entirely the fruits of his own invention. That he had found, and used, actual antient documents is unquestionable. Mr. Evans observes that Chatterton, in his account of St. Matthias's Chapel, afterwards Canynge's Place, talks of a Roman front towards Redcliff-street, and a Saxon front towards the river. Now the traces of a Saxon front have been discovered there, since his decease, on digging the foundations of a manufactory. It may be, likewise, remarked that many words and phrases used by Chatterton were said, by the best black-letter scholars who engaged in the controversy respecting him, to be words of his own fabricating, and such as were never used in the fifteenth century. But it has been since shewn that the words in question really were used by writers of the fifteenth century, although writers with whom the said critics were not familiarly acquainted. The inference is obvious. If the best black-letter scholars of the age, men mature in years, had not met with such modes of expression in all their extensive reading, is it likely that they should have been discovered in the printed authorities accessible to a youth of seventeen?

Mary Robinson, born in the Minster-house of the cathedral, Nov. 27, 1758.

Ann Yearsley, born in 1756. Mrs. Yearsley pursued the humble occupation of a milkwoman, but was introduced to public notice as the author of several poetical pieces, various in their degrees of merit.

Among our contemporaries may be mentioned the names of Southey; Dallaway; Lawrence; and Baily, the sculptor.

The view of the HIGH STREET is taken from the Bridge over the Avon. The second view is taken from the church-yard of St. Augustine. Looking over the shipping in the Floating Basin, is seen a part of the city ornamented with several towers and steeples. This view is thought to convey a due notion of the city in its mercantile and busiest districts.

37

Stoke-Bishop

THE SEAT OF SIR HENRY-CANN LIPPINCOTT, BART.

THE great beauty of the north-western environs of Bristol has been noticed in several preceding articles, and particularly in our accounts of King's Weston, Blaise Castle, and Redland Court. The parish of Westbury-upon-Trim, in which is situated the seat now under description, comprises much of these fine environs. It is distant from the city of Bristol about two miles and a half, and is bounded on the south-west by the river Avon. On the north and north-west it meets the parish of Henbury; and the little river Trim, from which it derives a part of its appellation, gliding through its verdant meadows, enters the Avon at Seamills dock.

Westbury attained, in past years, considerable celebrity from a collegiate foundation. It appears that a monastery existed here long before the conquest, but the date at which it was founded is not known, although it is mentioned in the Acts of the Synod of Clovesho, A.D. 824. It is memorable that King Edward III. presented the reformer Wickliffe with a prebend in the collegiate church of Westbury. Richard Duke of York, and his third son, Edmond Earl of Rutland, were eminent benefactors, and are erroneously termed by Sir R. Atkyns, the founders of this religious house. The establishment then consisted of a Dean and five Canons. William Canynges, Mayor of Bristol, renowned for his liberality to the church of St. Mary Redcliff, took on him the order of priesthood in 1467, and became Dean of Westbury. He was a great benefactor to this college, and is said to have re-edified the buildings. If so, it is much to be regretted that they are not now in existence, as, from his connexion with the church of Redcliff, it is probable that they were designed in an exquisite taste. They are briefly and unsatisfactorily described by Sir Robert Atkyns, as "having strong walls, with turrets at each corner, and on a large tower on the south side with battlements."

This establishment flourished until the general dissolution of monastic houses, at which time its annual revenues were at 232*l*. 14*s*. The fabric was entire early in the reign of Charles I.; but was chiefly destroyed in the civil wars, by order of Prince Rupert, to prevent its affording a garrisoned post to the parliament's army. Some few remains were incorporated, in the last century, with buildings forming the seat of the Hobhouse family.

This parish contains, among other subdivisions, the tithing of STOKE BISHOP, of which we have already taken some notice in our account of Redland Court. We may here repeat that it formerly belonged to the *bishop* of Constance, in Normandy, and was afterwards vested in the bishops of Worcester, by whom it was held until the year 1547. Dr. John Carpenter, consecrated bishop of Worcester in 1443, had so great an attachment to this place, that he is said, in Tanner's Notitia, to have sometimes styled himself bishop of Westbury. He was buried, according to his own direction, in the chancel of the church.

The estate on which the mansion of Stoke Bishop is erected, belonged to the family of *Cann*, through several descents. William Cann, styled of Compton, was an alderman of Bristol. Robert

STOKE-BISHOP

Cann was created a baronet by Charles II. in 1662. Sir Robert Cann, the last baronet of this family, died without issue, in 1765. This Sir Robert had an only sister, named Catherine, who married Mr. Charles Jeffries, of Bristol, and had issue one son and one daughter. Robert Cann-Jeffries, her son, succeeded to the estates of his uncle; but, dying a bachelor, the whole of his fortune descended to his sister, who, in 1774, was married to Henry Lippincott, Esq. created a baronet in 1778. The present Sir Henry Cann Lippincott, Bart, is the son of that gentleman.

The house of Stoke Bishop was erected by Sir Robert Cann; and, as is shewn by an inscription over the porch, was completed in 1669. A view of this structure, as it appeared in the early part of the eighteenth century, is given by Sir Robert Atkyns. It had then a court in front, enclosed by high walls. A broad paved foot-path led from the outer gate to the foot of the mansion, designed, as we have stated when noticing a similar path of parade at Cleve-hill, for the display of the dress and state of visiters, in days of formality and ostentation now happily extinct. Immediately beyond the outer wall ran the high road. The course of this road was thrown to a distance by Sir Henry Lippincott, in 1778, greatly to the advantage of the estate. On the right of the house were extensive gardens, laid out in square plots, and adorned with rows of trees and shrubs, flower-beds in whimsical shapes, and a *jet d'eau*. It will be seen, from the view inserted in the present work, that those gross violations of simplicity and correct taste are now removed, and that the grounds are disposed with a due attention to the natural charms of the place. For such, improvements Stoke Bishop is indebted to the first baronet of the Lippincott family.

This is a spacious, fine, and venerable mansion, highly, but not extravagantly ornamented. The most obvious feature in the principal front is the enriched porch, over which are two stories, terminating in a pierced parapet. It is observable that, in the character of the pediments in the same front, and in the coronal shape affected in the cupolas, we find a resemblance to the domestic style of architecture prevailing in the reign of James I. The interior is highly-finished, and displays much rich work, curiously exhibiting the fashion which prevailed in the time of the second Charles. The house underwent large repairs from Mr. Jeffrys and the first Sir Henry Lippincott; and those gentlemen deserve warm commendation, for the judgment they evinced in preserving, as regards every principal part, its original character. It is seated on a noble eminence, and commands varied views, in which the rivers Severn and Avon, animated by shipping, form captivating features.

High Grove

38

High Grove

THE SEAT OF JOHN PAUL PAUL, ESQ.

THIS handsome residence is situated near Tetbury, and is in the hamlet of Charlton, within the parochial limits of that town.

Sir Robert Atkyns traces the manorial property of Charlton back to the reign of Henry VI. Edward Mortimer, Earl of March, died seized of this manor, in the third year of that King. In the thirty-eighth year of the same Henry's reign, it was granted to Cicely, Duchess of York, for her life; and was confirmed to her in the first year of Edward IV. Catherine, queen dowager of Henry VIII. held it in dower; but, in the sixteenth of Elizabeth, it was granted to Drew Drury and Edward Downing. It was afterwards purchased by an ancestor of Lord Ducie; and is now in the possession of his lordship.

The mansion of High Grove was erected, a few years back, by John P. Paul, Esq. and is a substantial and spacious family residence. The design is entirely free from ostentation, although some ornamental particulars are introduced. The principal efforts of the architect have been directed towards the interior, which presents many good apartments of accurate proportions, well suited to the domestic and hospitable purposes of a family of high respectability. The situation is fine, and excellent views are obtained from the house and various parts of the attached grounds.

The present proprietor of this seat married, in 1793, Mary, daughter and sole heiress of Walter Matthews, of Battersea, Esq.; and, a few years since, served the office of High Sheriff of Wiltshire.

There are several marks of antiquity in the neighbouring country, and we believe that a barrow was lately opened in the vicinity of High Grove, but without the discovery of any curious articles of funeral deposit.

Newark Park

39

Newark Park

THE SEAT OF LEWIS CLUTTERBUCK, ESQ.

NEWARK PARK, called in the old writings Oslennorde, is situated in the parish of Ozleworth, two miles east of Wotton under-Edge, eighteen south of Gloucester.

Ozleworth was a Berewic or Member belonging to the manor of Berkeley, at the time of the general survey, as appears by Domesday-book, where it is said, that half a hide in Oslennorde belong to Berchalia. The manor was afterwards granted by the Berkeley family to St. Augustin's abbey, in Bristol, whose claim to a court leet was allowed the fifteenth of Edward I. The abbey of Kingswood in Wilts, was seized of Ozleworth the twelfth of Henry IV. continued possessed of until the general dissolution of religious foundations, when it was granted to Sir Nicholas Pointz, the thirty-first of Henry VIII. whose family was before seized of it as tenants under the said abbey of Kingswood. Of Sir N. Pointz it was purchased by Sir Thomas Rivet, alderman of London, and of whom it was purchased by Sir Gabriel Low, alderman also of London, and from his heir Gabriel Low, the estate was purchased by the late James Clutterbuck, Esq. from whom it descended to the present proprietor, Lewis Clutterbuck, Esq. who is patron of the living of Ozleworth, lord of the manor, and possesses more than half of the lands in the parish. Newark House, which stands on high ground, commands an extensive and beautiful prospect. It was built by Sir N. Pointz, out of the ruins of Kingswood abbey. Its former beautiful east entrance is still preserved. The house has been considerably improved, and a beautiful south front added, by the father of the present proprietor, under the direction of the late T. Wyatt, Esq. architect.

HILLFIELD

40

Hillfield

THE PROPERTY OF THOMAS TURNER ESQ.

IS a modern built house, situated in the North Hamlets, in the vicinity of Gloucester. It partly lies in the hamlet of Wotton, and partly in that of Kingsholm, upon an eminence, at the extremity of that portion of the latter, celebrated as being supposed to form a considerable part of the antient city of Glevum.

The opinion that the Kingsholm was placed within the compass of this city, so famous in the annals of antiquity, is strongly corroborated by the fact that coins, antiquities, and skeletons have been, and still are, frequently found in digging for gravel, throughout these fields. Of the former, very considerable numbers have been discovered, belonging to the early, as well as the later Roman Empire, and many have been obtained on the ground, upon which this villa is built.

Henry III. granted Kingsholm, then valued at eight pounds per annum, to Robert le Savage, to be held by the service of doorkeeper of the king's pantry. Through several other proprietors, the manor passed to the family of Beauchamp. It afterwards came to Rowland Arnold, Esq. who died possessed of it in 1573. This hamlet is now divided among several proprietors. Mrs. Mary Pitt, only daughter of the late John Pitt, Esq. M.P. for the city of Gloucester, and widow of the Rev. James Pitt, is the principal landholder, and owns the manor.

The hamlet of Wotton, to which we have alluded, is situated in the parish of St. Mary de Lode, but has its own officers.

Wotton House is the property of Mrs. Westfaling, of Rudhall, in the county of Hereford, widow, and is at present occupied by William Goodrich, Esq. of Maisemore Court, in the county of Gloucester. Wotton Court House is the residence of Mrs. Hopkinson, widow of the late Colonel Hopkinson, and his family is possessed of very considerable property in the hamlet.

The house and the grounds, of which we now present an engraved view, command beautiful views of Robin Hood's Hill, May Hill, with the high lands in the forest of Dean, the Malvern Hills, and the city of Gloucester; its magnificent Gothic Cathedral is likewise displayed in its most picturesque point of view. Immediately behind the house, the walks are perhaps as enviable as any in the vicinity of Gloucester, commanding, in addition to the above-mentioned features, views of Churchdown Hill, and the long range of the Cotswold Hills in the distance.

Mr. Turner has displayed his love of the fine arts, by collecting a few pleasing and choice examples of the old masters, in the Italian and Dutch Schools.

Christ and the Woman of Samaria. Pietro da Cortona.
St. Rosa. Carlo Dolce.
Infant Christ and St. John, with a Lamb, in a Landscape. Rubens.
Holy Family. Murillo.

The Angel appearing to the Shepherds. Karel du Jardin.

A Sea-piece (extremely fine.) Backhuysen.

A ditto, (Companion.) Vander Cassela.

A large picture, Cattle, with Herdsman, and the Town of Dort in the distance. Albert Cuyp.

A smaller picture, with many figures. A beautiful specimen of this master. The same.

A very fine picture by Vander Heyden, *with figures* by Adrian Vandervelde.

There are, likewise, in this pleasing collection, several landscapes and architectural interiors by Pynaker; Ruysdael; Wilson; Philip Wouvermans; Adrian Vandervelde; Metzu; and Terburg.

41

Eastington House

THE SEAT OF JOHN PHILLIMORE HICKS, ESQ.

THE parish of Eastington is situated about six miles to the west of Stroud, and nine miles to the south of Gloucester. It is situated in the Vale, and consists chiefly of rich pasture-ground and meadow, watered by the meandering flow of the river Froom.

The date at which Eastington became a distinct and independent parish has not been ascertained, but the descent of the manor may be traced as follows, with the aid of the account presented by Sir Robert Atkyns, and intelligence obtained from private sources. Winebald de Balun, son of Drogo de Balun, who entered England with the Conqueror, was possessed of this manor in the second year of William II. We find this Winebald styled, in 1126, one of the great barons of the realm. Sir John de Balun, a knight of this family, and lord of Eastington, joined in the rebellion of Simon Montfort against Henry III. and, in conjunction with Sir John Giffard of Brimpsfield, took Gloucester castle, by stratagem, in the year 1264. He afterwards obtained the King's pardon; and the manor descended to Isolda, his daughter, who married, as her second husband, Hugh de Audley the elder, who purchased a charter of free warren in Eastington, in the twelfth of Edward II. Hugh de Audley, his son, succeeded to this estate, and married Margaret, second sister, and one of the co-heiresses, of Gilbert de Clare, Earl of Gloucester, and widow of Piers de Gaveston, favourite of King Edward II. who was put to death at Blacklow Hill, near Warwick. Margaret, only daughter and heiress of the last named Hugh, married Ralph Lord Stafford.

Hugh, Earl of Stafford, son and heir of Lord Ralph, died at Rhodes, on his return from a pilgrimage to Jerusalem. He settled this manor, together with that of Haresfield, on Hugh Stafford, his younger son, who died without issue, leaving Eastington to his nephew, Humphrey, Earl of Stafford, created Duke of Buckingham in the reign of Henry VI. With the descendants of that nobleman the estate continued, until the attainder of Duke Edward, in the thirteenth of Henry VIII. It was then granted to Thomas Heneage and Catherine his wife, for life; but was subsequently (twenty-third of Henry VIII.) restored to the Staffords, in the person of Henry, son and heir of the attainted Duke. By Edward, Lord Stafford, son and heir of Henry, it was sold to Edward Stephens, Esq. in the fifteenth year of Elizabeth. In the lineal descendants of that gentleman it remained, until the decease of Robert Stephens, Esq.; when it descended, by will, to Henry Willis, Esq. a collateral branch of the family, who assumed the name of Stephens.

The building, of which we present an engraving, and which has been termed Eastington-house, is a capacious and substantial mansion, the seat of John Phillimore Hicks, Esq. It is agreeably situated amidst verdant grounds, much adorned by the gentle stream introduced into our view. It was built, we believe, by the family of Clutterbuck, who enjoyed considerable property in this parish, through several descents, and had two dwellings here, in the early part of the eighteenth century. The chief part of their property in this parish has been recently purchased, in addition to that which formerly belonged to the family of Stephens, by Henry Hicks, Esq. of the Leaze.

EASTINGTON HOUSE

The parochial Church of Eastington is a venerable structure, in the pointed style, with an embattled tower at the west end. The roof is of oak, with many traces of carved ornaments. Over the south door are the letters S. B. the initials of Stafford and Buckingham, having a ducal coronet between them. The same letters are frequently introduced in stained glass, as are also the armorial bearings of the Earls of Gloucester. Many of the family of Stephens are here buried, commencing with Edward Stephens, Esq. who died 1587, and Joan his wife.

BROWN'S-HILL

42

Brown's-Hill

THE SEAT OF E. P. CARRUTHERS, ESQ.

BROWN'S-HILL is situated in the parish of Painswick; one of the most delightful districts in Gloucestershire. The house is well adapted for the residence of a family of elegant habits, and contains several apartments, designed and finished in an excellent taste. The grounds are extensive, and are not more remarkable for their native beauty than for graces imparted by the temperate interference of art. One attractive feature in their disposal has been thus noticed by Mr. Fosbroke. "Upon the side of the park next to Painswick, from a peculiar felicity in the grouping of some fine full-grown trees, a beauty in park-scenery is created which cannot be surpassed. The group is of forest trees, not all equally and too close together, but irregularly scattered."

From the same writer we obtain the following particulars concerning the family of Carruthers. "William Carruthers, of Almaine, in Annandale, in Scotland, who fled thence for his adherence to James II. and settled at Stonehouse, married Mary, daughter of William Pawlin, Esq. of Brown's-Hill, and had issue John of Pitchcombe, and William, of Brown's-Hill. John married Ann, daughter of Thomas White, Esq. of Stonehouse, and has issue Marianne, only daughter and heiress, born at Pitchcombe, Sept. 9, 1786. William married Grace, sister of the above Ann, and left issue *Edward Pawlin*, eldest son and heir, born in 1789."

Traces of Roman buildings have been discovered at Brown's-Hill; and on Painswick-Hill is one of the *Castra exploratoria* of the Romans. On the last-named hill Charles I. encamped, shortly after he had raised the siege of Gloucester.

BRIMSCOMBE PORT

43

Brimscombe Port

THE canal-basin and wharfs thus denominated are on the Thames and Severn canal, and are situated at Brimscombe, a hamlet within the parishes of Stroud, or Stroudwater, and Minchinhampton.

In the year 1783, an Act of Parliament was obtained for a canal, to form a junction between the Thames and the Severn, obviously the two most important rivers in the kingdom.

The THAMES AND SEVERN CANAL commences at Walbridge near Stroudwater (where it joins the Stroudwater Navigation) taking an ascending and winding course, through that delightful vale which has acquired the appellation of the Golden Valley, to Brimscombe, a distance of two miles and a half. From Brimscombe it proceeds to Chalford, and continues to ascend until it reaches the summit at Daneway.

From Daneway is an uninterrupted level of nine miles and a half; and on this part of the canal is that noble work of art, the TUNNEL, which is conducted under Saperton Hill, and is designed for the passage of vessels nearly of seventy tons burthen. Its length is 3808 yards, or nearly two miles and one quarter. Through a part of this distance it is cased with brick and stone, whilst the remainder exhibits the natural rock, which from its variety of irregular forms, partially revealed by lights, presents a curious, and in some degree an awful, spectacle. It may not be superfluous to observe, that sketches from different parts of the interior have been made by artists employed as scene-painters to the theatres. This was the first tunnel attempted in England, on so large a scale.

Seven years were occupied in perforating this hill; and, as the greater part of the rock was removed by the application of gunpowder, many lives were unfortunately sacrificed. Twenty-four shafts, or pits, were sunk, for the purpose of drawing to the surface the excavated parts, the deepest of which is 300 feet. It is a remarkable circumstance, that, notwithstanding the great length of this vast aperture, it is so perfectly straight, that the opposite entrance can be distinctly seen by a person situated at either of its ends.

On this part of the canal is, also, a fine aqueduct, thrown over the turnpike road leading from Cirencester to the village of Kemble.

At Siddington, a village about one mile and a half from Cirencester, the level ceases, and the canal begins to descend towards the river Thames or Isis, passing, in its progress, the town of Cricklade, near which place, in the year 1819, a junction was opened into the Wilts and Berks canal, by means of which, boats, seven feet in width, and carrying about twenty-five tons, may proceed as far as Abingdon on the one hand, and Bath and Bristol on the other. From Cricklade the canal continues its course, through an open and flat country, to the village of Kempsford, and thence to Inglesham, near Lechlade in this county, where it terminates by entering the Thames, or Isis. The total fall from Siddington is 129 feet, on which are sixteen locks. The whole distance, in a direct line, from Walbridge to Inglesham, is twenty-eight miles and three quarters; which, added to the length of the Stroud Navigation (eight miles), makes the total distance from the Thames to the Severn thirty-six miles and three quarters. The locks from the river Severn to Brimscombe Port, are calculated to admit vessels 68 feet long, and 16 feet wide; and, from the last named place onwards, they admit vessels 90 feet in length, and 12 feet 6 inches in width.

At the distance of about half a mile from Brimscombe Port, are some valuable and extensive quarries of free-stone, of a very fine texture and quality. Considerable quantities of this stone are sent to various places, but chiefly to London, where it finds a ready market, as it is greatly superior to the free-stone of Bath and it may be remarked, that some has been used in the alterations now making at Windsor Castle.

The basin and wharfs represented in our engraved view, and known by the name of BRIMSCOMBE PORT, are spacious, commodious, and in every respect worthy of important navigation upon which they are placed. The basin is capable of containing one hundred vessels, of the sizes customary on this canal; namely, from twenty-five to seventy tons burthen: and the quays, wharfs, and warehouses are provided with every convenience for facilitating the trans-shipment of merchandise and coals, which operation is necessary, in consequence of the different descriptions of vessels used upon the respective rivers. It must be observed, however, that many vessels have been lately built on a construction calculated to prevent the trouble of unloading, and which enables them to convey their cargoes from the place of shipment to the port of their final destination.

The trade on this well-conducted and truly important canal is very considerable in coals, stone, slates, salt, and general merchandise.

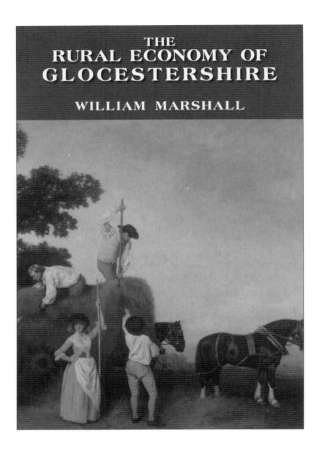

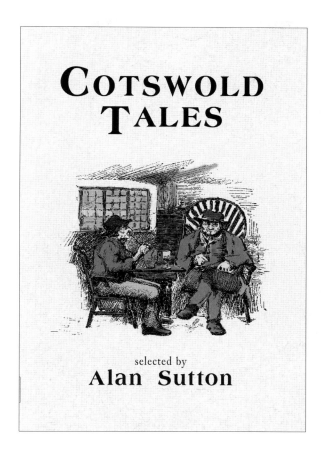

Collected tales about the 'ordinary' folk of the Cotswolds: their daily lives, the work they did, their traditions and customs and, of course, the stories they told. Gathered from contemporary sources, these four sets of tales tell of a way of life long since vanished.

£10   ISBN: 1-84588-014-5
268 pages, 56 illustrations

Also Available from Nonsuch Publishing

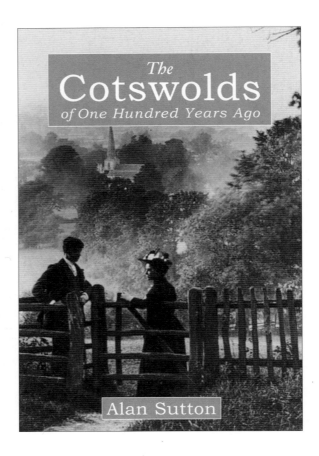

A selection of photographs of the Cotswolds as they
were a century ago, as well as images of the people who
lived and worked there, with stories and anecdotes still
strangely familiar to the modern reader despite the
passage of time.

£15   ISBN: 1-84588-053-6
160 pages, 150 illustrations